THE ROLE OF
THE INDIGENOUS AFRICAN
PSYCHE IN THE EVOLUTION
OF HUMAN CONSCIOUSNESS

THE ROLE OF THE INDIGENOUS AFRICAN PSYCHE IN THE EVOLUTION OF HUMAN CONSCIOUSNESS

Mike Loutzenhiser

iUniverse, Inc.
New York   Bloomington   Shanghai

THE ROLE OF THE INDIGENOUS AFRICAN PSYCHE IN THE EVOLUTION OF HUMAN CONSCIOUSNESS

iUniverse books may be ordered through booksellers or by contacting:

iUniverse
1663 Liberty Drive
Bloomington, IN 47403
www.iuniverse.com
1-800-Authors (1-800-288-4677)

ISBN: 978-0-595-50376-6 (pbk)
ISBN: 978-0-595-61481-3 (ebk)

Printed in the United States of America

Contents

Acknowledgments

I would like to thank Nyame, Kwabena Slaughter, Theresa Roth, Paz Lenchantin, Larry Goldberg, Jeffrey Young, the Boulder Public Library and everyone in the struggle.

In memory of Mark Loutzenhiser (1962–2006),
Luciano Lenchantin (1975–2003)
and Don Ohadike (1941–2005).

Preface

Regardless of our ethnicity or cultural orientation, we observe the achievements of Europe: monumental cathedrals which have existed since early A.D., incomparable militaristic advancements, cars, airplanes and satellites.

Indigenous people are usually depicted in the media and in popular academics as primitive pagans. Most people do not think about it consciously, but the fact that we are in a technological world today and indigenous people did not have very advanced material technology or, usually, written languages has great bearing on ethnological views at large. The main goal of this book is to reduce the misconceptions regarding ethnology and gender psychology, mostly in the field of transpersonal psychology. Today there are subtle forms of racism against blacks. A large part of this, I think, has to do with modern technology. The more we get caught up in technology the more primitive indigenous cultures appear to most people on some level. I think that the fact that most people are not interested in psychology, as a good example, corresponds to their obsessions with technology. I think that largely we have become this technological because of our (industrialized cultures') ignorance to psychology.

Asians developed in a manner similar to Europeans historically. They gave Europeans gun powder and, some say, domesticated horses. The Chinese produced many important inventions, including the magnetic compass (which revolutionized navigation), rocketry, the abacus (or first computer), the first map of the continent of Africa and the Bessemer process of converting iron into steel. (So much for Jared Diamond's well-known, subtly Eurocentric and Afrophobic enough paradigm, as presented in his book *Guns, Germs and Steel*, which is ardently embraced by, for example, *National Geographic* magazine.) Historically they have been centuries ahead of Europe on many basic empirical counts, yet, in the final analysis, psychologically they have historically been infinitely more similar to indigenous societies than to any colonialist or neocolonialist society (Roberts, 1999; Bond (Ed.), 1996). The first boat was apparently built in Japan, 10,000 B.C. Modern transpersonal psychologists like Eastern religions, i.e., Taoism, Buddhism, Hinduism. Most people, when they think of Native Americans think of Wakan Tanka. So, Native Americans are pretty much established in the modern white psyche as monotheistic. Also they have lighter skin than blacks; I think there is something to be said about this. Black, metaphorical shadows. Actually the color black is the sum of all colors, unlike shadows, which are the absence of color.

To this day popular scholars associate drums and rattles with primitives. Today at least 300 million people in at least five-thousand distinct indigenous cultures resist industrialization. *Nature Conservancy* magazine reported in '00 that eleven square miles of the world's rainforests were being destroyed each day and that at least three species were disappearing each hour.

I think that the most recent theories at the forefront of transpersonal psychology, by authors like John Nelson and Ken Wilber support, often inadvertently, the idea that most indigenous cultures had cosmological views that we are only now beginning to understand. Of course cosmological evidence will not be enough to reverse misconceptions at large regarding indigenous cultures, nor will common explanations of indigenous ecology. As long as Europeans are popularly viewed as materialistically incomparable (though this is not the view of any insider), the idea of ethnic equality will remain insufficiently supported in popular academics. Europeans were not empirically superior (let alone incomparable), nor more intelligent (or conscious). Evidence of this fact is irrefutably documented (Du Bois,1915; Herskovits, 1958; Parrinder, 1973). This involves the contexts of material advancements and of religious practice, cosmology, philosophy, psychology, linguistics, mythology, socio-politics, architecture, surgical techniques, agriculture, metal smithing and other crafts, economics, taxonomy and aesthetic views. In the study of all areas of traditional African culture modes of materialistic consciousness are not separable from African cosmological views. Material developments and socio-political interaction in traditional Africa all stem from religious and cosmological aspects. White scholars have not understood this because their own traditions have not had this quality and/or because of stratification, for various all too explainable reasons, in historical academics or, of course, because they are simply racists. In this book I will go into these and other subjects in the context of comparisons of indigenous to industrialized cultures and explicate some of the basic facts beneath the myths. I will try to reveal both the crudest and the most intricate myths concerning these topics and to meet their propagators on any valuable academic grounds that have been proposed.

The historical, materialistic (or empirical) developments of Africa have been described in plenitude by definitive authors whose names and contributions to our understanding of Africa I could exhaust indefinitely. What have not, I think, been adequately presented (by black or white scholars) about the traditional African psyche are its religious and philosophical ideas as they pertain to modern, transpersonal psychology. A thorough treatment of these subjects and their relation to each other will be the main thrust of this book, and they will be addressed often in reference to the work of Ken Wilber. The basic reasons for the latter mode of investigation are three in number, and they are all inter-related. 1) I am convinced that traditional African philosophy is particularly phenomenological, perhaps moreso than any other traditional philosophy in the world; 2) Wilber has done more than any other living author of psychology to support basic principles of phenomenology and 3) Wilber has also devised the most elaborate Eurocentric theory of the evolution of human conscious-ness. This is originally somewhat confusing. If Wilber is such a great phenom-enological philosopher why has he put African and other indigenous cultures below industrialized cultures? Also, G.W.F. Hegel—who Wilber considers to be one of the greatest philosophical geniuses in the history of European phi-losophy and whose work I will discuss throughout this book—himself was a racist, as is thoroughly documented in his *The Philosophy of History*. (It should be noted that Kant also produced a racist philosophy of history.) Some schol-ars, like Clinton R. Jean in his *Behind the Eurocentric Veils: The Search for African Realities* (1991) have even accused Hegel of being the prime source of Eurocentrism in white academics.

On one hand I simply want to explain African philosophy better than has been previously done. On the other, I do not want people to interpret Wilber's hegemony as reflective of either African culture or of the intrinsic value of Hegelian phenomenology. I will be referring to different aspects of phenome-nological-existentialism and its historical appearances intermittently through-out this book.

There were two displacements of Africans and African Americans: the original displacement from Africa when 11 million people were brought to the Americas as slaves, and the second displacement, which coincided with the Emancipation Proclamation in 1863 (Canty, 2000). When trauma occurs the effect is an emotional block between ones limbic system and their frontal lobe, which makes it difficult to think clearly. There are, really, myriad factors that are rarely considered by either ethnically biased scholars or by those who are particularly interested in ethnic equality. Most scholars have a narrow attitude about this. Some of them, who are otherwise brilliantly integrative, have all but failed to do any justice to the vital proponents of wisdom made available by indigenous cultures at large and historically.

This book began as a series of notes mostly regarding phenomenological aspects of modern transpersonal psychology. At this point it was influenced by psychologists such as R.D. Laing, Carl Jung, Ken Wilber and John Nelson and other scholars such as Hegel, Martin Heidegger and Hans-Georg Gadamer. There was sparse, related information that I wanted to make available to the public at large. It occured to me that, while modern transpersonal psychology was making progress on many counts, no one had the whole picture. The one who came closest to having the whole picture, in my opinion, was probably John Nelson. I agreed with some of Laing's "antipsychiatric" concepts. Wilber, on the other hand, had, in my opinion, done the most to clarify numerous ideas regarding existential phenomenology, with ideas such as the pre/trans fallacy and the ladder paradigm. Jung had supplied a large amount of clinical research regarding precognitive dreams, the principle of synchronicity, divination, the anima and animus, and so on, which are all conducive to forms of indigenous cosmology (or psychology). He gave valuable anthropological accounts of indigenous people in one of his two last books, *Memories, Dreams, Reflections*. He was also a close friend of Laurens van der Post for sixteen years. Van der Post, known for books like *The Heart of the Hunter* and *The Lost World of the Kalahari*, wrote the definitive biography of Jung, *Jung and the Story of Our Time*. Nelson was apparently the only author in the field of transpersonal psychology who had an incisive understanding of the chakra system. It was, in fact, nothing short of amazing. He was also relatively fluent regarding fifth chakra (or metaphysical) matters, i.e., many of those that Wilber supports and, in some instances, has pioneered.

The idea was that all of these accurate aspects needed to be catalyzed, and it was clear to me that much more needed to be added, before and after their integration into a single, cohesive system. I noticed that these psychologists who had done much work that I admired often fell short of understanding compatible aspects of "other" systems, including indigenous systems. Wilber did not understand some of Jung's best contributions. Jung did not understand Hegel, even though their systems were profoundly compatible. Jung noted similarities between his own spiral paradigm and Hegelian phenomenology. He basically thought that once the collective unconscious was established the ontology became "redundant." Wilber did not understand how compatible Jung's spiral paradigm was with his ladder paradigm and Hegelian phenomenology.

This was the first strata; I wanted to marry the authentic view of the chakra system, as described by Nelson, with authentic metaphysics, i.e., Wilber's ladder paradigm (based largely on the work of Hegel). I wanted to integrate both of these with Jung's ideas about synchronicity, precognitive dreams, the anima and animus and much of depth psychology in general, and some of Laing's "antipsychiatric" views, which were really nothing other than a socio-politically insightful application of phenomenological-existential philosophy.

The second phase of my research constituted a process of finding the scattered reservoirs of related knowledge. I discovered that Anton Wilhelm Amo, who was born sometime around 1700 in Akonu, Ghana and died sometime around 1767 and who was brought to Europe from Ghana—given as a gift to the Dukes August Wilhelm and Ludwig Rudolf von Wolfenbuttel by the Dutch West India Company in 1707—and who taught and studied in Halle, Wittenberg and Jenna, Germany from 1727–1747, developed a system of metaphysics that is perhaps closer to the systems of Hegel, Pierre Teilhard de Chardin, etc. than any other non technically phenomenological-existential system in the history of European philosophy. His system is presented in his book, *Treatise on the Art of Philosophising Soberly and Accurately*. Leopold Senghor, the main theorist behind the Negritude Movement, said that in terms of historical European philosophy Teilhard de Chardin's system—which was particularly similar to Hegel's—was closest to the traditional African world view. Aime Cesaire, who coined the term *Negritude* in his epic poem *Notebook of a Return to the Native Land*, was a Hegelian. Then there is Frantz Fanon—who is well-known for books like *The Wretched of the Earth*. His system seems to be basically phenomenological-existential. I discovered that Cornel West is, as were W.E.B. Du Bois and Martin Luther King, Jr., a Hegelian. West has called Hegel "the most adroit philosopher."

West being probably the most celebrated black intellectual in the United States, Du Bois being the first black person to get a PhD from Harvard and one of the fathers of sociology, and King being one of the greatest leaders of any passive resistant movement in history, the fact that they were all Hegelians struck me as particularly profound.

Then, there was the surrealist movement in Europe. I had been interested in surrealism, for lack of a broader term, art and literature for eleven years, particularly in its expressions in Latin America and the Caribbean (the most Africanized part of the Americas). These were where the greatest surrealist artists and poets seemed to come from. I had already formulated many ideas about surrealism by this time, but I needed to research its expression in Europe. This yielded astounding results.

The first surrealist manifesto was written in 1924, the second in 1929. The European surrealists, led by Andre Breton, have been widely misconstrued in popular academics. This is partly the fault of the surrealists and partly because of the fact that their ideas, once they had matured, were too sophisticated for most scholars to understand. They were slow to formulate their philosophy.

The first manifesto emphasizes "psychic automatism" and the "superior real-ity of the dream." This was their first stage. And, in fact, some of them had seen ahead even then. Pierre Reverdy and Paul Eluard being perhaps the two best examples. Surrealist philosophy in its most developed stage in Europe was an innovative synthesis of Hegelian phenomenology, Freudian free association and what Jung would later call depth psychology. This was made explicitly clear in the Second Surrealist Manifesto. Breton and the rest of the group singled out Hegel as their primary philosophical influence (Balakian, 1986; Benedikt, 1974). This is not an overstatement, as much as it has been overlooked. Members of the European surrealist group at the time of the publication of the second man-ifesto and/or after included Tanguy, Tzara, Duchamp, Man Ray, Dali, Bunuel, Picabia and other prominent figures. They were all, during their memberships, in perfect allegiance with Breton's overall ideology, and they all signed papers testifying to this fact. The surrealists were interested in the authentic dialectic between dreams and the waking state. Even in 1933, the year that Breton wrote his best essay on automatic creativity, titled *The Automatic Message* (four years after the second manifesto), Breton and other surrealists in Europe explained in articles and interviews that they were still formulating many of their ideas. But these were important and prolific ideas.

One of the most significant points regarding their admiration of Hegel's work is that most of them had a reverence for indigenous cultures. They were largely uninspired by the state of music in Europe and were almost unanimously fans of jazz (Rosemont, 1978). In conjunction, Breton, Max Ernst and others were close friends of Claude Levi-Strauss, the inventor of structural anthropology, who coined the term *bricolage*, what he called a form of "combinatorial logic," an advanced system of dichotomization employed by most indigenous cultures, based on what Jung would later call the principle of synchronicity. The surreal-ists generally, like Laing, associated the psychological sophistication of indig-enous people with that of children, the opposite of what Wilber proposes. This is a complicated subject, which I will address in detail in the book.

In *Man and His Symbols*, Jung's other last book before his death, Jung gives a good account of the European surrealist movement prior to the second mani-festo. Here we have an interesting phenomenon. See, Wilber doesn't mention surrealism in any of his books. He mentions Breton on only one page of *The Eye of Spirit*, and it is an inexplicit reference. The surrealists were Hegelians like Wilber, but unlike Wilber they did not believe that technology equaled supe-rior consciousness or that ancient indigenous cultures were predifferentiative or premonotheistic and so forth. Jung had more in common with Hegel than either he or Wilber realized. The criticisms that Jung made about the European

surrealists in *Man and His Symbols* were all correct in the context of their ideology prior to the Second Surrealist Manifesto (1929), but these same criticisms were particularly akin to basic tenets of Hegelian philosophy, which the
surrealists after the second manifesto supported exhaustively (Balakian, 1986;
Benedikt, 1974). Here we have an entire movement, which originated between
the first and second World Wars, which has been neglected historically by popular psychology. Psychology is the only field capable of explaining the philosophy of the European surrealists.

Aside from this there seems to be a disconcerting ratio of prominent black
Hegelians to prominent white Hegelians. By emphasizing the role of Hegelian
phenomenology in European philosophy and philosophy of European extraction I am not trying to narrow down the possibilities of human individuality,
as it might seem to some readers. It is evident to me that Hegel's work was the
philosophical equivalent of the cubism of Braque and Picasso, or Nijinsky's *The
Rites of Spring*, or Elvis' rockabilly. Wilber has called the European rediscovery of cubism "evolutionary," but he considers its ancient form, what might be
called classical cubism, to be primitive. His work is full not only of blatant contradictions but also many harsh, ethnologically biased remarks. One example,
"primitive people don't seem to have logic." I mean, try taking this statement
out of context. Likewise, when there is a remarkable degree of gender balance
in indigenous cultures, which there often is, Wilber generally attributes it to
predifferentiation.

One of the areas that I will focus on most is the general connotations of
material technology as it pertains to the evolution of human consciousness.
Another is the relation between what Wilber calls "cyclic" and "accumulative"
consciousness. Wilber suggests the distinction between "cyclic" (indigenous)
cultures and "accumulative" (industrial) cultures. I think that most indigenous
cultures where cyclic and accumulative, that the integration of both is vital to
any psychologically healthy way of life, or any culture in the most applicable
sense of the word. I think that industrial societies are generally only accumulative and that this is contiguous with the fact that they are generally, to an equal
extent, premandalic. This is only part of "the tip of the iceberg," as it were. I will
address this and many related factors of ethnological stratification in popular
academics throughout the book.

Considering Amo, the Negritude poets, Fanon, Du Bois, King, Laing, West,
the entire European surrealist movement, et al. Wilber would do better to go
with the ethnological flow, especially if he wants his Hegelian views of the hierarchy to be adhered to. With Wilber what we have is one of the most insightful
phenomenologists in written history and the most popular living psychologist.

Given these facts at least half of his readers should be reading Hegel and/or the phenomenological hermeneutic philosophers. This is not happening. Only the minutest percent of his readers read Hegel. Most of his readers don't understand anything about the hierarchy; which is to say the pre/trans fallacy or the ladder paradigm in general. Anyone can investigate this for themselves by going to any University library and researching the number of times definitive books by or about Hegel or the phenomenological hermeneutic philosophers have been borrowed in the last twenty years. It is obvious that most people who understand existential phenomenology support ethnic equality. Wilber doesn't.

I think that this threshold and that of any authentic, judicial investigation into matters of ethnology and gender psychology exist on a mutual plane. I mean this in general, including but not limited to cosmological factors.

If we look at Linda James Myers' *Understanding an Afrocentric World View* (1993) we can see that while she uses the words "ontology" and "epistemology" throughout the book in reference to ancient African cosmology she does not understand their meanings on a genuinely metaphysical level. What she ends up with is a pseudo-metaphysic, basically identical to what most ecologists, feminists and new agers subscribe to today, which became popular with the appearance of the hippie counter culture in the sixties. The view that Myers applies throughout her book is bereft of any well-defined hierarchy; it does not distinguish clearly between levels of consciousness. The reason, as usual, is that it is difficult to address the interconnectedness of nature and the hierarchy of consciousness at once. Most scholars see the two concepts as mutually exclusive. As Wilber has said, these ecologists, feminists and new agers while trying to illustrate the web of life, which does exist, gut the same concept of its innate proponents which are necessary to any voluble description of it, namely, the hierarchy of consciousness. Myers does discern ethical actions and ideologies from those that are not ethical and she explicitly promotes the integration of unity in diversity, but she does these holistically rather than in the context of a complete metaphysic.

Most people in industrialized societies today are much further removed from any complete metaphysical philosophy. One of the reasons for this, I think, is that people who have an excess of material luxury are more prone to solipsistic and structural deterministic complexes, etc. Another is that whatever consciousness made us stray originally from the indigenous path, the path of the dialectics of ecology, existed in the same vein as that which would nine hundred years later be responsible for the release of atomic energy. The same type of consciousness that was never able to tell the difference between biochemistry and electro mechanics.

Understanding the psyche individually or collectively is not something that can be put on the back burner.

So, the subject of monopantheonism is one of the simple and important aspects of ethnology that must be rationally addressed. It can also be addressed metaphysically. And I will address it metaphysically in some detail. Thereby we will see that all of the metaphysical cards are absolutely stacked against Wilber's misconceptions as well. But there is another equally simple part of ethnology which has been (and is) as neglected as the monopantheonism issue. This other part is materialistic. Most people who say that they believe in ethnic equality are not looking at the validity of empirical comparisons between cultures. By this I mean developments in architecture, agriculture, linguistics, crafts (such as metal smithing), surgery, taxonomy and so on. This is a necessary means of comparing cultures. Few people know that there were hundreds of stone buildings built in sparse regions of ancient Africa from the Cape of Good Hope to the Sahara, from Nubia to Zimbabwe. Few people know that the North West Planes Indians, who lived in a climate and natural environment similar to that of Norway developed their architecture similarly to how people in Norway did, on a similar time-line. People rarely know that in various tribal regions of Africa indigenous surgical techniques were practiced that were sometimes more advanced than those practiced by Europeans at the respective times. More commonly people are aware that numerous nonindustrial people had languages that were more advanced than those of their European conquestors. Few people are aware of Levi-Strauss's rediscovery of *bricolage*, what he called "a form of combinatorial logic," which most indigenous people used. Some of the Anasazi cliff dwellings contain more than two-hundred rooms. Toward the end of the colonial era paramount linguists emerged from every basic ethnic group. Between the Emancipation Proclamation in 1863 and 1941 at least forty-three African Americans are documented to have received Doctoral degrees in all major subjects, often from the most renowned schools, including Harvard and Princeton. Nomadic cultures are generally, semi-consciously considered primitive. In reality, many of them were among the most profound and powerful societies that ever existed. While many people say that they believe in ethnic equality and many of those people might support ethnic equality in their own rights, few of them are rationally comparing industrial and nonindustrial societies in the contexts of religion or materialism. In the final picture a profound and simple metaphysical mask moves into view, that of ancient indigenous people.

CHAPTER ONE

Metaphysics

The oldest ethnic group on the planet is the most violently oppressed ethnic group on the planet ... The connotations of this fact in regard to the metaphysical consciousness and overarching syllogistic thought (logic/reason) expressed by the black diaspora is a subject that I will address in multifarious conjuncting ways throughout this book. It is no doubt one that lends itself to dynamic transformation in academia in general, to the degree that many otherwise progressive scholars are against the unveiling of types of ancient and traditional African syllogistic reason that particularly reveal the traditional African identity.

Today metaphysics in the European academic tradition is by and large defined—frankly, very crudely—as that area of science or philosophy that deals with "ultimate truths" and so on. Metaphysics is most functionally defined as that area of philosophy or science in which that which is outside a given subjectivity (or the immediate conscious perception of a given individual) is integrated (In oversimplified but more or less accurate terms, this is the establishment of what is called in the European academic tradition the *ontology*.) and from there one reasons about the connotations of the existential relation between the subjective and the objective (In the European academic tradition this is called the *epistemology*.).

The nature of—syllogistic—reason, when it is applied consistently, is such that, as historical philosophers—from Socrates to Aristotle to Plotinus (having preserved at least some ancient African metaphysical knowledge)—have said, metaphysics—in the most functional sense of the word—*integrate and transcend* strictly empirical science.

This basically metaphysical approach to the sciences and academia in general is expressed in the concept of what Aristotle calls "first science". It is expressed in the concept of what Plotinus calls the "virtue of Wisdom" versus the "natural virtues," etc. But it originated in ancient Africa, assumably tens of millennia B.C., as there is no pervasive evidence of there having ever been any basic change in the brain structure of *homo sapiens sapiens* since our appearance, cir. 100,000 B.C or earlier nor any substantial evidence that the collective, what we would call in psychological terms, *sense of temporality* of the human species has become any greater since our appearance. On the contrary, even internationally renowned scholars like Octavio Paz, Carl Jung, Martin Luther King, Jr., Alan Watts, Bertrand Russell, Houston Smith and Michel Foucault have said explicitly that European scholarship has been regressing metaphysically for a number of centuries, which inarguably connotes that the collective sense of temporality of the human species has, overall, decreased.

In fact, clearly the middle-class, bourgeois and even non-lumpen proletariats in the First World, collectively, are thoroughly solipsistic, violently dissociative of the *other*.

The truth is that the scholars who run the academic show dictate what history is supposed to be but cannot get Herodotus'—the earliest Greek historian—work basically right per se. Herodotus (1928) says that the Egyptians during his time—fifth century B.C.—were "dark-skinned and wooly-haired." He writes of Ethiopian Egyptian kings, et al. *He and other ancient historians testify explicitly that the ancient Greeks learned a huge amount of what they knew about metaphysics, mathematics, et al. from the Egyptians, that ancient Greek culture was basically weened on ancient Egyptian culture and that the ancient Egyptians were predominantly black and Africoid.* For example, Aristotle writes on page two of *Metaphysics, which is ostensibly one of his more popular opuses,* "… the mathematical arts were founded in Egypt; for there the priestly caste was allowed to be at leisure."

Herodotus' work has been around for about 2500 years. And the historians who are running the show cannot get his work basically right. *This is the reality. This academic situation is mirrored by mainstream and, for all means and purposes, popular philosophy and psychology at large.*

Aristotle's "First Cause," the "Unmoved Mover," for example, sounds a lot like a Creator that is referred to in texts from throughout dynastic Egypt. In an Egyptian sun-hymn from cir. 1500 B.C., for example, there is mention of a "Fashioner without being fashioned." (This is similar to what is referred to in ancient Taoist scripture as "That which gives birth" but is "not itself born." Et al.)

G.W.F. Hegel says in *Lectures on the History of Philosophy vol. 1* (1995), "The doctrine of the transmigration of souls extends even to India, and, without doubt, Pythagoras took it from the Egyptians; indeed Herodotus (II. 123) expressly says so. After he speaks of the mythical ideas of the Egyptians as to the lower world, he continues: '*The Egyptians were the first to say that the soul of man is immortal*, and that, when the body disappears, it goes into another living being; and when it has gone through all the animals of land and sea, and likewise birds, it again takes the body of a man, the period being completed in 3000 years." (My italics.)

Considering these factors, it is difficult to say with that much precision—without greater knowledge of technicalities of ancient Egyptian metaphysics than I possess—what sum of metaphysical expressions in the works of Plato, Aristotle, Plotinus, Aquinas, et al. are essentially more or less expressions of Kemetic (ancient Egyptian) influence (Obenga, 2000, *et al.*).

This chapter is the most dense one of the book, and the beginning of this chapter is the most dense part of the book. I am trying to appeal to peoples' rationales, but I am trying to do this in a way that moves in the direction of an overall infinitely more integrative and holistic world view than what we see in popular European psychology, anthropology and so on.

Establishing some basic idea of what is happening with the globe's historical and contemporary expressions of the supernal philosophy is a task to reckon with, especially when *the Eurocentrists who run the academic show are generally far from really understanding even, say, the metaphysics of Socrates* (who never wrote anything). It is true that even prominent historians of philosophy like Paul Tillich and Kwame Anthony Appiah distort the history of European philosophy considerably. (In Appiah's work, for example, probableism, which contradicts itself as soon as one tries to assert that it is true or even probably true, is subscribed to, phenomenology is defined as that area of philosophy that does not deal with objective truth, *et al.*)

In short, it seems, in the final analysis, to be best to start primarily with the subjects of historical and contemporary European metaphysics, at least largely because most of the people who read this book will have some sort of European educational background, but also because *it will be necessary to obtain a functional overview of what is happening with historical and contemporary European philosophy and psychology in order to decipher what has happened/is happening with various factions of the human species psychologically, comparatively*, and for other reasons.

The use of European terms like *supernal philosophy, phenomenology, subjective* and *objective* in this book is at least largely due to my own linguistic limitations, etc. Beyond what I have said I will not address any latent accusations of assimilation here. They would, in any case, only be coming from those who choose to exoticize Africans, as though rationale is not a prerequisite for higher states of human consciousness.

In *functional metaphysics* we get beyond any latent solipsism immediately with the use of the word *objective*. In *strictly empirical science* we can talk about sub-atomic particles or astrophysics and say that we know these things to exist or be true *objectively* and at once not be certain that anything exists outside of ones own subjectivity. (Certainty in historical, contemporary and even prehistorical philosophy and views of the psyche, self versus other, etc. is a subject that I will address frequently—though often vicariously—throughout the book. As I will show (much to the dismay of legions upon legions of armchair philosophers), it has always been infinitely more popular among the oppressed—people in the Third and Fourth World, etc.—than it has been among mainstream or, by and large, popular scholars.)

As W.T. Stace writes in *The Philosophy of Hegel*:

> "Reason the subject of the logic, is on the one hand the system of objective categories, and on the other hand it is the system of those subjective categories or concepts by means of which we do our think-ing. Objective and subjective reason are identical, and the logic is therefore the science of both. As the science of the objective reason, the absolute, the supreme reality, it is an ontology or metaphysic. As the science of subjective reason, of the categories with which we think, it is an epistemology. Kant's list of categories is only an epis-temology because he regarded the categories as purely subjective. Hegel saw that the categories are objective as well, so that his account of them is also a metaphysic, or ontology. And lastly, since it is the science of human, ie. subjective, reason, it is also, in the usual sense of the term, a logic."

Metaphysics, on any level beyond that of (metaphysical) physics, actually consists of several components, which can be divided a few different ways. There are for example a number of ways that the ontology can be presented. Depending on which of these ways is employed the epistemology can run various courses. All of these ontological methods and their available episte-mological counterparts are (as respective combinations of ontologies and epis-temologies) functionally equal to each other.

What we establish with the presentation of any phenomenological ontology (I will refer to *phenomenological-existential* systems—in the tradition of Hegel, Pierre Teilhard de Chardin, Martin Heidegger, etc.—as simply "phenomenol-ogy". This is distinct from Edmund Husserl's *transcendental phenomenology*.

(Heidegger's system is usually associated with Husserl's, but it was actually much more similar to Hegel's. Heidegger didn't read Hegel's work until after he wrote *Being and Time*, etc.)) is the fact that we are through corresponding epistemological symbols able to reveal objective content. In Hegelian phenomenology, unlike Kantian and other similar forms of philosophy, the entire basis of the reason is that we can reveal "content," that reason corresponds to, effects and is effected by that which is beyond reason. That which is beyond reason (or perception) has two basic types. I call these the *relatively objective*, that which is simply beyond immediate perception; and the *purely objective*, that which is beyond perception entirely. Both types of objectivity are established by way of the ontology. And they are both prerequisites to the procedure of any phenomenological epistemology.

The ontology, in itself, establishes systematically nothing effectually more than what I have described in the preceding paragraph. Within the epistemology, however, from whichever direction it is addressed, several key principles are eventually embodied. All of these key principles support each other. In turn, in order to master the explanations of any of these principles one must have a complete understanding of all of them. Here is a list of some of these principles in no particular order:

1) Because all finite factions are interconnected, one cannot help any of these factions without helping all of them.

2) The entirety of time and space exists within each finite faction.

3) In order for polarities to be balanced there must be something beyond polarities to balance them.

4) When polarities lack balance they lack that which is beyond polarities to an equal degree.

5) Every polarity is equatable to its opposite.

6) Finite space is a substrata of finite time, thus time and space are infinitely equatable.

7) Everything finite has a polarity.

These phenomenological tenets are perhaps not clear to those who are not familiar with metaphysics, but they are by way of Hegelian phenomenology all interrelated with each other. They support each other intrinsically, and any of them can be used to explain any of the others. All of this coincides with why we call metaphysical thought "mandalic consciousness" (Ken Wilber's term).

Holons as Contiguous with Metaphysics

Time and space each have two aspects. One is holonic. The other is non-holonic and pertains to time and space equally. It is shared by both and is the same aspect for both, namely that which is independent of physicality. This is identical to what Plotinus describes in Tractate II from the third Ennead, *Province*. Holons, by definition, consist of both a physical (material) and a non-physical aspect. The latter component is spiritual and thereby infinite.

The non-holonic aspect exists in terms of the automatic equation of the entirety of holonic space to the entirety of holonic time. Both space and time in their entirety, as consciousness, are not restricted; thereby they are both non-holonic.

In order to understand the non-holonic equation between the two we must first understand how the two equate holonically. In their holonic forms space is a sub-strata of time. Time is represented as a potentially infinite number of lines progressing vertically. Space is represented as a potentially infinite number of horizontal lines reaching from one end of holonic time to the other. Holonic time refers (dialectically) to any stage of time's progress. By this I mean any stage of time's explication into consciousness. The explication of either time's entirety or the entirety of space into consciousness marks the end of both holonic time and holonic space. More precisely, it is the catharsis of both, the redemption of their physical properties.

This fully explicated state of time and space constitutes an aperspectival consciousness which is not dependent on the finite, material world.

It is important to note that throughout the progress of holonic time (and space) they are both intrinsically conscious. This is what is meant by dialectically bringing to light what is. Everything is already conscious. It is only a matter of becoming conscious of consciousness. We have again the diad of intrinsic consciousness and the lack of perception of that consciousness. Likewise, while all is one, there is also separation. Neither cancels the existence of the other. The mechanics of this are somewhat intricate and can only be understood metaphysically.

There is that boundless consciousness which coexists with the finite. This consciousness, by definition, is not dependent on the finite; whereas everything finite does depend on infinite consciousness. This infinite consciousness is what I call pure objectivity, in contrast to relative objectivity, which is—like all subjective states—finite, or at least entails finite components. (I will clarify this later in this chapter.) When we have the coexistence of infinite consciousness and finite factions (The latter being potentially manifest in a number of basically different psychic structures.) there is the constitution of holonic existence. When all of the finite aspects of all holons are explicated into consciousness we have the transcendence of the necessity for metaphysics.

Metaphysics is necessary to the catharsis of the finite components of holons in general. This is why Ken Wilber coined the "pre/trans fallacy." Although the infinite, on one level, coexists with the finite, we are no less responsible for explicating into consciousness that finity. In metaphysics the ontological existence of finite components of the cosmos is exactly what we base our epistemology on. It is not as though we are saying that we're not sure that anything finite exists or that we're not sure that there is a difference between the finite and the infinite. For those to whom that stance applies—metaphysically, we view them as speaking prematurely. It does not make sense to say that one is not sure that a problem exists and at the same time speak as though they are an authority on the problem. In phenomenology we first recognize that there is an ontological problem, then, because of what this ontology intrinsically connotes, we come to optimistic conclusions about the possibilities of resolving those problems. This optimism is based on the natural, syllogistic (mandalic) order which the ontology affords. But in order to understand this mandalic order we must first have the dignity to admit that there is definitely a question to begin with. Off-color terms have been applied to this approach, "absolutist," "laborous" and others. Despite whatever criticisms there might be toward the phenomenological view, it works. Popular ideas such as cause and effect cannot be volubly explained without phenomenology, which frustrates its critics all the more. They do not like the idea of certainty, often attributing it to arrogance and so forth. At the same time, *without addressing the subject of finiteness as a static, ontological point from which to draw dynamic, epistemological conclusions none of the ideas which the supernal philosophy embodies can be volubly explained*. We end up with contradictions at the end of every otherwise theoretically accurate road and so on. A lack of epitomic distinctions would be fine if there was a lack of epitomic problems in the world or if the human psyche did not have finite components. Since, however, there are people starving in Somalia, since there is environmental destruction, since there are innocent people imprisoned in the world, racism, sexism and myriad other problems, we cannot say, *Well, maybe these problems exist, but reason, by definition, cannot shed any light on them*. We must, in order to supply an entirely consistent epistemology, think in terms of a static basis.

Wilber's pre/trans fallacy, consisting of two fundamental types, ptf-1 (reductionism) and ptf-2 (elevationism), is of paramount importance to the understanding of any, what he calls, "complete metaphysic." The pre/trans fallacy is not, however, the final indicator of whether or not a particular system of logic is a complete metaphysic. Some systems—i.e., Carl Jung's spiral paradigm—are, contrary to Wilber's claim, not suspect to the pre/trans fallacy.[1] At the same time these systems which I am referring to are not complete forms of metaphysics either. Carl Jung states that it is necessary to explicate the collective unconscious into consciousness and that by doing so something "new" and "perhaps more important" is "created." In this sense he did escape ptf-2, which Wilber accused him of, but, as I say, his system was not a complete metaphysic.

There are three books in which Jung referred to Hegel: *Psychological Types*, *The Structure and Dynamics of the Psyche* and *The Symbolic Life*. Although Jung founded transpersonal psychology and contributed a great amount of important theories, it is clear from his references to Hegel, if not from the inconsistency of his overall body of work, that his system had no conscious basis in Hegelian phenomenology. He was partial to Kant rather than Hegel. It was because of that exact disposition that Jung never formulated a complete metaphysic.

When we have scholars like Jung who have neither constituted a complete metaphysic nor committed any type of pre/trans fallacy, what we always end up with is a system of logic which is somewhat metaphysical and, at once, not altogether consistent or usually accurate. There are also latent obscurities. This generally happens at what John Nelson in his book *Healing the Split: Integrating the Spirit into our Understanding of the Mentally Ill* (1994) describes as the upper fourth chakra. Other renowned figures who fit into this category include Plato, G.W. Leibniz and Plotinus. (Without straying from the present subject, metaphysical influences in fourth chakra consciousness, I should mention that I will be using Nelson's model of the chakra system throughout this book. I will explain why as I proceed.)

With figures such as Jung, Plato, Leibniz and Plotinus we have metaphysical ideas which are not sufficiently supported within those corresponding bodies of work. Jung's idea of the collective unconsciousness existing outside of the duality of the conscious and unconscious psyche was metaphysical. Plotinus' idea of holons was metaphysical. Leibniz idea of the relations between "symbols" and "things" was metaphysical. But none of these scholars understood phenomenology, thus none of them were able to fully explain their ideas.

---

1   Wilber's paradigm, for all of the invaluable metaphysical ideas expressed in it and all of the acclaim his work has received and does receive, is thoroughly Eurocentric and patriarchal. He explicitly denies this, but it is an irrefutable fact. See, for example, the lower right quadrant of his Four Quadrants paradigm—which is in the front of a number of his books—where he places tribal societies two and three distinct hierarchal levels below industrialized societies. I will address Wilber's hegemony and that of other prominent scholars in this and the proceeding chapters.

Likewise, many scholars have tried to adopt previously founded, upper fourth chakra ideas without understanding phenomenology with disastrous results.

Earlier I said that I would clarify what I mean by "the finity that all subjective states either consist of and/or entail." Subjective states are usually finite in themselves. There is an exception when we have certain aperspectival subjective states. There are a total of two basic types of aperspectival subjective states: holonic and non-holonic. The holonic type is what I mean by subjective states that entail finity. Non-holonic states are a completely different matter. I will address those in the next section. Holonic, aperspectival consciousness (subjectivity) is unconsciously finite. It is because it is unconsciously finite that it is often mistaken for a type of ultimate enlightenment. The fact is that while such states of consciousness do occur and can best be categorized as types of satori (or minor enlightenment) they do not constitute the ultimate transcendence of the ego. They essentially consist of aperspectival, egoic awarenesses of the complete interrelatedness of all finite parts. The ego is still there and thus the unconsciousness as well, but one is temporarily unconscious of the fact that there is a seam between ones ego and any other holonic faction. These experiences have some validity. They are in their own right transrational, but they are states of consciousness which can be attained without the degree of discipline necessary to the complete transcendence of the holonic aspects of the psyche. Likewise one always returns from these states of satori to face his inherent metaphysical responsibilities.

There is—holonically—a gap between what is and what is brought to light, which is none other than the gap between each individual's consciousness. More precisely, it is a gap between the consciousness of each given individual and that of each other.

The unexplicated consciousness of the individual remains complete and thereby non-holonic throughout all of the stages of holonic explication. A holon, however, while existing in metaphysical accord with the progress of the collective is not necessarily unto itself conscious to any degree in the explicated sense. We are, however—when we say dissolving the gap between the consciousness of each holon and every other—referring specifically to the explicated consciousness of these individual holons.

Because every holon progresses through time in direct accord with every other holon in existence at any given stage of (both collective and individual) spiritual evolution, we can assert that each holon eventually develops some degree of explicated consciousness. Given that this consciousness—which we will call i.c. (individual consciousness), since it is the only form of consciousness that is ever limited in scope—is eventually born to each holon, there must be (at some point) a degree of i.c. assigned to each holon which every other holon can work with. Since no single holon completes its evolution immediately, it is not necessary for our rationalism that holons attain an initial degree of i.c. immediately.

What I have described is a basic overview of metaphysics. As I shall illustrate this sort of logic is the basis of various forms of philosophy the world over, from Taoism, Buddhism and Hinduism through Hegelian phenomenology, including the later phenomenological hermeneutic philosophers such as Heidegger and Hans-Georg Gadamer.[2] Unlike Wilber and Schelling I do not think that Plotinus' completed the invention of holons. Nowhere in *The Enneads* does Plotinus' "mixed thing" qualify as a functional holon. In order for the holonic model to function one must include the three psychic components that, as Wilber has stated, are necessary to any "complete metaphysics." Leibniz' relations between "symbols" and "things," even without holons, were in some ways more functional in the direction of a complete metaphysic than Plotinus' most mature work was. In my opinion Plotinus' work is often one-sided, ambiguous and full of unnecessary capitalizations. I don't think that he surpassed the Greeks who preceded him by 600 years. But Neoplatonism (the genre that Plotinus belonged to) was progressive in many ways, especially with their principles regarding the importance of sympathy.

I consider Jung to be an unsurpassed psychologist in his own right. He has done an incomparable amount of work to help us understand the nature of mythology, precognitive dreams, systems of divination and the psyche in general. One of the aims of this book is to help integrate most of his basic views into a complete metaphysic.

It is often thought that the sensory is confined to the physical and that the mental transcends and includes the physical. In the human psyche there are three basic components: sensory (the unconscious and the emotions), symbolic (the perceptions, the consciousness) and spirit (that which transcends the duality of the former factions). If consciousness can be dialectical, then we cannot call that consciousness bereft of spirit. It must have an emotional, unconscious counterpart. Therefore the sensory is not always confined to the material

---

2   I think that Hegel's work was considerably more developed than Schelling's (despite being based on Schelling's and the two of them being close friends). Heidegger would later refine Hegel's work to a staggering degree.

either. What is without spiritual influence can only be material. Because of this we know that the mental can be material unto itself.

When there is spiritual (dialectical) consciousness it is not material. It relies on a spiritual, emotional counterpart, and these spiritual emotions rely on spiritual consciousness. It is basically a cyclic relationship between the two. We also see from this that the sensory aspect (which we call the soul) is no more potentially physical than the symbolic aspect. Thereby, as I will show more thoroughly in the second chapter, dreams do not exist at a higher level of the psyche than events in the waking state do.

Wilber has also keenly stated that physics can only represent the first level of metaphysics because it does not explicitly explain the three aspects of the psyche which are necessary to any complete metaphysic. Without taking into account these three aspects (sensory, symbolic and spirit) we cannot explain vertical evolution or the hierarchy, and empiricism is thus only transcended mathematically—at best. However, rather than initially calling purely mathematical metaphysics incomplete, I prefer to simply call it non-psychological.

In Nelson's *Healing the Split* metaphysical consciousness, which is basically ascribed to at the fifth chakra, is described as the consciousness of "the creative genius." While it can be argued that creative genius exists prior to attunement to the fifth chakra, I definitely agree with Nelson that if there is any single chakra that creative genius can be associated with it is the fifth. He also gives a particularly comprehensive account of the differences between this and lower forms of syllogistic reasoning, especially in the section titled *Fifth-Chakra Thinking and Logic*—barring his statements about synergy, since an awareness of synergy can be attained at as low as the third chakra. Nelson, though a paramount psychologist in my opinion, loses volubleness when mentioning examples of fifth chakra individuals. He mentions figures such as Freud and Kant who were not fifth chakra.

The psychologist who has the most exquisite understanding of fifth chakra consciousness since R.D. Laing is Wilber. Here is a quote from *Eye to Eye*, "In the second phase of the return of Spirit to Spirit, or of the overcoming of self-alienation, development moves from (prepersonal) nature to what Hegel calls the self-conscious stage. This is the stage of typical ego or mental awareness—the realm we shall be calling personal, mental, and self-conscious. [...] Finally, according to Hegel, development culminates in the Absolute, or Spirit's discovery of Spirit as Spirit, a stage/level we shall be calling transpersonal or superconscious." The "pre/trans fallacy" is based on (in terms of European philosophy) the work of Hegel, essentially. As I have said these ideas are necessary to any full understanding of holonic theory.

Wilber has illustrated metaphysical thought as exhaustively as any psychologist in history. The only psychologist that I know of who is equal to him in the area of fifth chakra consciousness is Laing who was writing over a decade before him. Wilber has managed to cover a lot of ground that Laing did not, especially in terms of integrative philosophy. There also are many points that Laing made that Wilber has still not come to terms with. I will reveal some of these later in the book.

The spiritual components of the sensory and symbolic areas of the psyche begin at the fourth chakra. Not all fourth chakra consciousness is explicitly dialectical, but the potential for a degree of dialectical consciousness begins there. It is the first altruistic chakra. Congruently it is where one eventually begins to outmode empirical reasoning.

Even sciences such as astrology require an understanding of the three components of the psyche to be practiced fluently. In astrology ones subjectivity is most represented by the natal sun and mercury, in that order. The natal moon represents the unconscious, the emotions and the ethereal body of the individual and so on.

Metaphysics is also known as mandalic consciousness. It is ultimately the basis of the supernal philosophy, and the only form of logic other than empiricism. It has many expressions from various regions. All of these are facets of the same mandalic consciousness. They have been introduced by figures such as Lao Tzu and Siddhartha, then people have turned them into traditions, then from these traditions various sects have emerged. This generally misses the point, which is that it all intrinsically amounts to the same supernal philosophy. Lao Tzu left his students on a yak because none of them understood him. Hegel was popular during the end of the nineteenth century, then he suddenly went out of style. Throughout history people have gravitated towards different forms of supernal thought, but they have rarely understood any of them.

The fact that everything is one does not mean that if one person is at peace, the rest of the world is too. It means that if one faction of the world is suffering then everyone in the world is equally responsible to heal that faction. This is known as *worldcentric* consciousness. As Wilber has shown, first consciousness is *self-centric*, then it is *sociocentric*, then it is *worldcentric*.

If you say that there is no suffering, and I say, "How do you know?" you can't really explain it syllogistically without also stating that there *is* suffering. Likewise both division and non-division must be recognized. Without suffering (or division) there is no dichotomy. Without a dichotomy there is no possible epistemological explanation. One simply cannot speak volubly about the mechanics or functions of the human psyche without conceding that there is an existential basis (ontology). If there's no dichotomy, there's no division. If there's no division, there's no question to answer. Without an original question there is no means to be rational. One cannot base a syllogistic argument on the idea that there is no right or wrong. Without right and wrong there is no point from which to begin the discourse, nor any direction in which to take the argument. There must be a static point from which to draw dynamic conclusions. If there is no right or wrong then nothing is correct or incorrect, so there's no reason to criticize anything. Criticism should be left to those who believe in right and wrong to begin with. Any stance prior to this would be pre-mandalic.

Mandalic consciousness is more syllogistic than empirical reasoning because empirical reasoning tends to blatantly ignore ontology. One word I will not use in reference to the supernal philosophy that almost every other writer of the supernal philosophy, including Wilber and Alan Watts, has is paradox. Paradox infers a contradiction. There is no contradiction in functional metaphysics. Therefore the word paradox is misleading in my opinion. What we have are truths that seem to oppose each other but do not. In Tibetan Buddhism these are called "coemergent wisdoms."

For example, the Four Noble Truths of Buddhism cannot all be simultaneously supported without metaphysical thought. Without the same tenets that are expressed in Hegelian phenomenology one cannot syllogistically say that "There is suffering in the world" (the First Noble Truth) and that "The path of right action leads beyond suffering" (The Fourth Noble Truth). So, we see that in metaphysics chronology is secondary.

I also will not cater to notions such as the Big Bang theory. It is based on strictly empirical science and thereby does not suit the metaphysical question which it claims to answer.

I do want to say that Albert Einstein and David Bohm have not been given enough credit. In physics quantum originally meant, basically, a unit of energy—which was in allegiance with the Greek etymology of the word. With Neils Bohr the idea of quantum became far more abstract. Bohr thought that, because of certain experiments, objects did not exist unless we were looking at them. Einstein's answer to this was, "I shall never believe that God plays dice with the universe." Meaning that he believed in a divine order.

He was the premier metaphysical physicist and the father of modern physics. Astrophysicists still use his theories to discover new frontiers of outer space. Wilber, in *Quantum Questions*, does not recognize Einstein's thorough awareness of metaphysics in all of its fundamental forms. He compares Einstein to Spinoza. Actually Einstein's physical paradigm has a lot in common with phenomenology. His math is not a complete metaphysic. That would be impossible. But he has conveyed an inimitable understanding of complete metaphysics in numerous essays. In *Einstein the Life and Times* he is quoted as saying, "Science is metaphysics." A keen statement, since fifth chakra consciousness is what all science eventually evolves to. As I have said, even purely mathematical metaphysics is mandalic.

Bohm, Einstein's closest colleague who went on to write literary metaphysics, has done wonders to defend Einstein's true scientific aims against the pirates of empiricism. His most valuable book in this right is perhaps *Causality and Chance in Modern Physics*. He points out how certain figures throughout history have caused empirical trends and misunderstandings.

In Einsteinian physics we have the fourth dimension, which represents the unity of time and space. Philosophers from Plato to Hegel have acknowledged that everything happens within time and space. So, there's really no way to dismiss the profundity of the fourth dimension. It basically represents the unity of everything in the physical world. The other part of Einsteinian physics is relativity. This shows how everything finite exists in relation to everything else. In other words, what effects one part of the universe effects all parts. The fourth dimension is not relative, because it is not finite. Thereby the fourth dimension does not depend on the relative, whereas the relative—because it is finite—does depend on the fourth dimension. As a basic view of the supernal philosophy this is accurate. Implicitly it defines the mechanics of the psyche. For this reason it is important that Einstein's singular contributions are recognized.

Wilber proposes that nonindustrial people have proto-superegos and proto-subjectivity (bicameral mind), and he forms numerous noncohesive theories to support these claims. This view of his is stated most explicitly in *Up From Eden*, and it is based largely Julian Jaynes' *The Origin of Consciousness in the Breakdown of the Bicameral Mind*. On one hand Wilber's ideas of mythology are thoroughly inconsistent with virtually everyone else's, including Jaynes', because he claims that sun and sky symbolism and hero myths all originated in Europe and the Near East. On the other hand Jaynes is much worse than Wilber because his idea of normal, healthy consciousness is the state of having an imbalance between the two cerebral hemispheres and his idea of unconsciousness is having a perfect balance between the two hemispheres. According to the bicameral theory nonindustrial cultures, because they supposedly do not have superegos, mistake voices which are compound structures of the voices of physical authority figures, i.e., Chiefs, parents and so forth, for the appearances of gods. Wilber claims that these cultures, which appeared about 12000 B.C., were the first humans, that hominids prior to this rough date were subhuman. These subhumans he calls "typhonic". The first humans, nonindustrial people generally, he calls "mythic-membership". Jaynes' theory states that hominids did not have egos prior to the second millennium B.C. So, according to Wilber the first humans were preegoic but they did possess praxis or verbal communication (which defines humanness), which constitutes what Wilber calls a "transorganic" or "supraorganic" level. According to Wilber praxis had emerged from the typhonic realm but not to the egoic level.

There are not more "typhonic" images in nonindustrial mythologies than there are in industrial mythologies. There is not less light symbolism nor fewer myths involving the slaying of the typhon. None of these comparative absurdities were ever objectively connected with totemism either. Nor are there fewer anthropocentric themes in nonindustrial societies. By no extension can the theory of the bicameral brain be supported anthropologically or otherwise.

There was no bicameral mind, and verbal communication is not necessarily transorganic. There is no ground, phenomenological or otherwise, to suggest that anything is transorganic other than spirit. There is only matter and spirit.

Everything symbolic comes from or through the sensory level. If symbolic level manifestations are spirit they come from spirit through the sensory level. If symbolic level manifestations are matter they come directly from the sensory level.

Whatever elements of the psyche are to be identified metaphysically must be identified in terms of either matter, spirit or both. Likewise if an element of the psyche is not spirit it does not constitute vertical evolution. Both vertical evolution (transformation, transcendence of any of the levels of the ladder) and lateral translation of level structures are spiritual. More precisely translation can occur in regard to distortion without spiritual, psychic elements. This material translation, however, unlike spiritual translation does not lead to the integration or transcendence (transformation) of any level.

Even at the prerational (or preegoic) chakras (one and two) vertical evolution can only occur by way of spiritual translation of the level structures local to the individual. Otherwise we would have to assert that spiritual evolution can occur, at least under some circumstances, without spiritual translation. This would be impossible. Spirit produces spirit, and matter produces matter; one does not produce the other. Of course there is the transrational causal level (Causal here does not refer to causality in the sense of its existence in the relative universe.) from which, according to apparently transrational sources, matter was originally created and from which karma is dealt in accordance with the universal laws of cause and effect. This is another subject, however, and one that I am not particularly anxious to write about or debate, since it regards the transrational, the realm of yogis and Mahatmas, not the realm of writers like myself per se. In the relative universe, which includes chakras one through five and the beginning of sixth chakra consciousness, spirit produces spirit and matter produces matter. One never produces the other.

The closest thing to a bicameral mind is third chakra consciousness because at the third chakra, where most people in industrial societies are, one can channel spirit but one is not generally aware of spirit consciously. The third chakra is the first egoic chakra, but the first altruistic chakra is the fourth. Nelson has also stated this. So, when spiritual activity occurs in the third chakra psyche, unless there are exceptional higher chakra influences, the individual is not consciously aware that these activities are spiritual rather than mundane. These spiritual qualities, in other words, are generally not integrated into egoic awareness at the third chakra. Morals, ethics, worship, genuine awareness of the principle of consubstantiation and so forth are not considered egoically at the third chakra unless there are exceptional higher chakra influences. To a significant extent this fits Jaynes and Wilber's description of the bicameral mind. Most likely the theories of the bicameral mind, proto-subjectivity and the proto-super ego are all projections of repressed third chakra influences.

Furthermore, complex technological consciousness can be third chakra. Human cloning is no doubt a good example of this. The subject is egoic, pre-altruistic consciousness. A large percent of state-of-the-art nano-technology fits the description of third chakra consciousness, not fourth or fifth. Even the philosophy being used by the engineers to support human cloning is clearly myopic (the idea is that human clones are not human, that they are a new type of organism). What is worse, human cloning or living in thatched roof houses? In my view nuclear warheads are not in any way a reflection of higher consciousness than that disposed to simple organic living. I believe also that this can be proven largely by way of the implications of Wilber's theories. There is only one egoic, pre-altruistic level of consciousness, the third. This makes the assessment of human material developments in relation to the consciousness of the respective individual fairly simple.

Phenomenologically we can identify what is ethical and what is not. What is ethical promotes the evolution of consciousness. While Wilber ultimately refers to the "solar-ego" (the level supposedly immediately after the mythic membership level) as a transformation or transcendence of the lower levels, there is one passage where he contradicts himself on this exact point: "As the organism dissociated into the egoic pole and the somatic pole, both poles were deformed. Not transformation, but deformation—and there is our topic." (Wilber, 1981). He also sides with Jurgen Habermas in saying that the problem today (especially in sociological and psychological theory) is that we use praxis to communicate from levels 3/4 to levels 1/2.

The difference between industrial and nonindustrial societies is that industrial societies continue to pursue whatever means possible to conquer whatever they can. This usually manifests as a futile and temporal dominance of levels one, two, three, four and five. Industrial societies, being as fervent as they are in third chakra, materialistic pursuits, aim to control anything at the egoic or preegoic levels. Nonindustrial societies did not generally have this problem. Their priests were often fifth chakra or higher, which means that most members of these societies must have been at the fourth chakra. Even if, hypothetically, nonindustrial societies were not beyond the third chakra, there would still be no ground to think that industrial societies were more conscious. Praxis obviously connotes egoic consciousness. Egoic consciousness can be pre-altruistic (third chakra) or altruistic (fourth and fifth chakra). There are no other options. Any society that regards its elders as wise, that distinguishes between pathology and shamanism and so forth is basically altruistic. There is not much of either of these elements in industrial societies and never has been. The increase in material technology, which began about 2500 B.C., was the product of a faction of greedy, third chakra Europeans. It does not reflect the entire evolution of the consciousness of white people per se, because white people, historically, have done as much as any other ethnicity to promote consciousness. The point is that the written word, materialistic inventions and so forth are, and have been historically, nothing more than third chakra translations. If we look to medicine, black people have made paramount contributions since the earliest period. They discovered many of the first vaccines. They have produced pioneers in the development of plastics, x-rays and so on. There is no "white man's medicine". I will address technological developments by blacks in detail in chapter three.

Jaynes is right that subjectivity and consciousness are (in their best hermeneutical usage) synonyms. He is also right that learning (and thus thinking) can occur unconsciously. Neither of these ideas are really new. There was Franz Brentano's idea of consciousness as intentionality. And Cecil Taylor, as one example, has spoken about the cognitive (unconscious) learning process as it applies to music.

Basically, in conscious beings intuition occurs invariably as part of the thinking process. Intuition is of the sensory sphere (unconscious), but it is, by definition, on the verge of becoming symbolic (conscious). In some instances the intuition can function as a means of cognitive learning while for numerous potential reasons not being allowed to emerge as consciousness.

Only beings capable of consciousness are capable of intuition. But the traditional African conception of consciousness (and that of perhaps all basic organic cultures) lends itself infinitely more to the understanding of the evolution of consciousness in general. Statements by Jaynes like "Lo! the very act of judgement that one object is heavier than the other is not conscious." absolutely miss the point. The consciousness of the weights of the objects comes from intuition, so does the comparison of the weights and the verdict of which is heavier. But consciousness and intuition are woven together in the process of judging which object is heavier. We can even, under different conditions, judge the weights of the objects (cognitively) without actual consciousness. This also would be both a learning and a thinking process, though unconscious. But many of Jaynes' postulations about the potential role of the unconscious in learning processes are not valid, and none of those that are cohesively support his theory of the bicameral mind.

There is much to say about Jaynes work as it pertains to the animal psyche, but as soon as we have language skills, as apes (especially bonobos), dolphins and some birds do, we have a certain level of object constancy. This is to say that some animals actually have consciousness (or subjectivity). Consciousness is, contrary to Jaynes' opinion, a thing. Consciousness is analogous to space, but space is not merely a process, therefore neither is consciousness. Space can be holonic or nonholonic, and consciousness can be aperspectival. Object constancy is contiguous with memory. By this I am referring exclusively to the type of memory that denotes consciousness. There is no basis for the idea that one can be capable of mimesis or considerable language skills without possessing consciousness. If people during what was supposedly the bicameral era did not have memories as humans today do they would not have been able to build or carve central architectural structures that faced the rising sun on the autumnal equinox as in Giza and Angkor Wat. Also Jaynes compares physiological unconsciousness, as in states of hypnosis, to the type of preconsciousness that supposedly exists in bicameral people, but in states of hypnosis ones memory is often exalted.

The point is that when consciousness is involved in the learning process the learning process itself is invariably best described as conscious. Preconscious learning is simply cognitive development. Infants for example have a particularly limited amount of object constancy, but they are bursting with potential for consciousness. All of the qualities of an adult mentality are not that far under the surface of their psyches. Mature egoic and (usually) spiritual influences are poised to be explicated. The infant is full of consciousness (usually spiritual). It is mostly within the sensory sphere, but it is no less valid.

Irene Josselyn (1971) writes, "In the early stages of embryonic growth the embryo looks not unlike a mulberry. It would be impossible to point to one cell and say that that cell will develop into an arm, another into a leg, another into the torso. Inherent in the total embryo, however, are all of these and many other physical structures."

Unlike Wilber, Jaynes says that the Iliadic mind was primarily bicameral, that they "did not have subjectivity as do we."

Mimesis in both painting and sculpture first appeared, as anthropologists conclusively know, no later than 30,000 B.C., tens of thousands of years prior to what we might call classical cubism. Object constancy is absolutely necessary for mimesis; thus wherever we have mimesis there is consciousness. Since bonobos and dolphins are conscious (have explicitly evident faculties for object constancy) and are yet incapable of mimesis we can assert that wherever mimesis appears there is egoic consciousness. Children are egoic and yet not capable of mimesis until at least the age of five.

All of this is pertinent to our discussion of the bicameral mind because it is popular among Eurocentrists, including Wilber, to compare infants and children to nonindustrialized people. Thus, all of the claims that nonindustrialized people are premonotheistic, preegoic and so forth typically apply vicariously to infants and children.

If we look at the time line between 100,000 and 30,000 B.C. (the latest that mimesis could have possibly first appeared, conservatively speaking) and we consider the tools that were used by hominids during this 70,000 year period, we can see that material developments increased gradually. *Homo sapiens sapiens* were like hatchlings in their nest. It was enough to simply accept the fact that they had egoic consciousness at first. Then there was fire, then drills and projectile weapons. Each of these inventions must have seemed overwhelming to early humans at the time that they occured. Each flap of their wings was a miracle to which they had to adjust. Eurocentrists like Jaynes, Wilber and Feuerstein write as though birds do not have wings until they fly half-way around the world. I think that this analogy states my argument fairly well. This also corresponds to the many pronounced forms of inconsistency in regard to their interpretations of mythology and related subjects.

According to Jaynes the first depictions of "angels" were in Assyria at the end of the second millennium B.C. He describes these as "the beginning of hybrid human-animal beings," "always part bird and part human." He continues, "But soon even this is abandoned." He states that by the beginning of the first millennium B.C. there were depictions of other hybrid beings including people with "the heads of birds" and "winged bulls or winged lions with human heads." This is the opposite of Wilber's claim that typhonic symbolism preceded the depiction of angels.

Jaynes says that in none of these depictions of angels does there appear to be an auditory (or vocal) transaction taking place. It is now a silent relationship between humans and divinities, and he says, "Because the personal gods are silent, they must be angry and hostile." These are, in Jaynes' conception, the first depictions of angels; and, according to him, they were contiguous with both the origin of mythology and of demons.

These winged, anthropomorphic animals are exactly what Wilber calls typhonic. And, according to Jaynes, they were preceded in the Near East by classical angels. The reason for this inconsistency is that the language of mythology and that of dreams are, as Jung and Campbell have said, for all means and purposes, identical. While it is not wise for people to imitate animals excessively (This can potentially have a regressive effect.), naturic symbolism in mythology, as in dreams, can be clearly revelatory. In fact, it can reveal what are otherwise physiologically unconscious (cognitive) thinking and learning processes, ie., those described by Jaynes. It can also be more sympathetic without compromising reason.

We can also note that, by Jaynes' definition, angels never appeared in the East. There are no winged anthropomomorphic figures in Buddhist or Hindu mythology. There are halos; but, interestingly, in the East all of the chakras were depicted, not only halos. This is particularly uncommon in European and Near Eastern religious art. This is an important difference between European and Indo-European mythology and that of the East. Whether we interpret halos as the fifth, sixth or seventh chakra the point is that whatever part of the psyche was below the halo was dissociated in the West and not in the East. Congruently, Campbell (1988) has said that Christianity is the only religion in the world whose adherants conceive of eternal damnation. Actually, it seems to be only in exoteric Christianity and Islam—which, it is very likely, are the most patriarchal, pre-mandalic, et al. religions that have ever existed—that people subscribe to concepts of eternal damnation.

There are several half animal gods in Hinduism. The most popular examples are probably Ganesh the elephant god (god of wisdom) and Hanuman the monkey god (god of language), but there are others, including a lion god and an eagle god. Even today there are tribes and animal sacrifices in many parts of India, from Bengal to Benares, and there are numerous animals, both literal and mythological that are considered divine in India. At the same time, there are many depictions of Hindu gods defeating what Wilber would call typhonic creatures. We have supposedly contrary presentations of the relation of humans to nature existing in equally pronounced ways on the same time-line. I remind the reader that the Tibetan pantheon is based on the Hindu pantheon.

I am not trying to defend the practice of animal sacrifices or the worship of half animal divinities. What I am saying is that if subscribers to Hinduism (which is similar in ways to many nonindustrial religions) can produce refined metaphysics, so can organic cultures.

The unique postulation of a hell did not parallel any transformation or original emergence of consciousness. This is why all insider and other definitive anthropological sources testify explicitly to the ethics (familial, socio-political and ecological) of traditional Africans.

The depiction of winged humans did not connote the origin of mythology. Nor were either the solar logos or hero myths more prominent in European or Indo-European myths. One can look at hundreds of pictures of African sculptures of humans without seeing a single anthropomorphic animal. Jaynes' views of early written language, from the hieroglyphs of dynastic Egypt (at least 3000 B.C.) to the Iliad (some time between 1230 and 850 B.C., according to Jaynes. And again, Jaynes says that Iliadic people did not generally have consciousness. At the same time he locates the collapse of the bicameral mind in Assyria about 1380 B.C. This is his description, "And what an empire it is! No nation had been so militaristic before. Unlike any previous inscriptions anywhere, those of middle Assyria now bristle with brutal campaigns."

One of the most important precursors to this supposed emergence of consciousness, in Jaynes' view, was the singular degree of commerce practiced by the Assyrians by 1950 B.C. This is a travesty because, as anyone who has studied indigenous cultures extensively knows, both Africans and Amerindians are extremely renowned for their economic genius and the geographical range of their commerce. It is also a fact that most of their trading was done peacefully. The Hopi, for example (whose name means peace) were involved prominently in trade throughout most of both of the Americas (below Canada). The expansion of commerce can easily parallel an increase in consciousness, but—contrary to what these Eurocentrists are saying—the escalation of war cannot.

Jaynes groups together possession, hypnosis, schizophrenia, poetry and music as partly remnants of the bicameral mind. It is difficult to oversimplify this postulation. Basically, he associates war primarily with consciousness and poetry and music primarily with unconsciousness. And if learning is, as he says, better described as "organic" than "conscious," then consciousness obviously has not increased our capacity to learn. Consciousness is not a mere process. There are not constant gaps in it. It is not limited in operation to "objectively observable things." There is no evidence that, by unconscious means, one can create architecture, art, social structures and so on that we have commonly, historically identified as products of consciousness.

African Philosophy

To address African philosophy I will begin with the subject of rhythm. Rhythm is the root of music, and it is, at once, not limited to sound. It manifests symmetrically in all types of form and motion. The degree to which one dissociates the role of rhythm in any context is the degree to which that individual dissociates the emotional aspects of their own psyche. The cardio-respiratory system is not particularly melodious; it is rhythmic. Somehow white hegemonists have failed to take this into account. If one wants to be in tune with the pulse of their physical or spiritual being they must turn to rhythm. Walking is rhythmic. Intercourse is rhythmic. One can also associate rhythm with battle. The clashing of swords or firing of guns is rhythmic. These are elements of existential reality. We cannot grow beyond these elements if we are dissociating them. It is a dialectic between the conscious and the unconscious mind. To have melody without rhythm connotes psychosis, while to have rhythm without melody connotes innocence.

Beyond this, discursive thought is potentially expressed much more vividly by rhythm, namely, polyrhythm, than by melody. Melody without rhythm is like a painting without lines, a boat without ores or a mind without a heart. Traditionally, throughout Africa polyrhythm was expressed more prodigiously than it was in any other culture. Rhythm in traditional Africa was not merely beating on drums. It was dialectical. And polyrhythms are not necessarily merely adding one rhythm to another. There is complex metering involved. We have one rhythm, then we add another, then another. We can do this indefinitely. Each individual has a rhythm and a synthesis is established between these rhythms. A single rhythm can appear and be maintained through diverse expressions. Through these diverse expressions one must be able to keep track of the same innate rhythm. Then we add another rhythm which is treated the same way, another, indefinitely. And all of these rhythms, through their changing outer forms, are harmonized with each other. This is about as discursive as music gets. This is the principle that all forms of African American music are based on, from the blues, to swing to bop to funk. Prior to jazz white people did not have this type of rhythm to any comparable extent. Mozart would not have been able to write his amazing compositions if he had not understood this type of polyrhythm. We can hear a certain expression of it in his work, the number of notes and so forth, but his music didn't really swing.

Rhythm is the ground on which the sky rests. We are trying to explicate the unconscious into consciousness, but we cannot do this by ignoring the unconscious. We must pay attention to dreams and visions. An individual could be a genius at dialectics and, at the same time, something could be happening in his life that he is not immediately able to rationalize. This is where attunement to the unconscious comes in.

This even pertains to accumulative logic in a sense. One ignores the value of rhythm to the extent that they ignore the value of their own instincts in dealing with new situations. Thus to underestimate the value of rhythm is to underestimate the possibility of new things occurring and to underestimate the importance of being able to adapt to new existential realities.

In most indigenous African cultures, instead of investing themselves comparably in material gain, they concentrated on psychological and cosmological harmony within the society and for the individual connectedly. They understood that to maintain harmony and psychological health required that they put those issues first. To assure that there would not be individuals exempt from productive roles in society was a full time job, and many indigenous people knew it. Because they concentrated first and foremost on maintaining social harmony and psychological health they appeared to European conquestors (who did not share those qualities) as primitive.

While Africans demonstrated an exquisite ability for materialistic achievements (every bit comparable to that of Europeans of the time), they were not overly materialistically fervent. This, rather than connoting inferior intelligence, as has been/is the popular myth in white texts historically and today, was due to their psychological sophistication.

In contemporary African philosophy there are basically two camps—the professional philosophers—also known as the universalist and nationalist-ideological philosophers—and the ethnophilosophers.

The four main proponents of professional philosophy are Paulin Hountondji, Kwasi Wiredu, H.O. Oruka and Peter Bodunrin. Proponents of ethnophilosophy include myself, Don Ohadike, T.U. Nwala, J.A. Umeh, Achille Mbembe, the Negritude poets, apparently all of the prominent members of the National Association of Black Psychologists (ABP, which I will discuss later in the chapter), various contributors to brilliant anthologies like *African Philosophy: New and Traditional Perspectives* (Brown (Ed.), 2004), Placide Tempels, Janheinz Jahn and Robin Horton.

Bodunrin writes (1981), "… ethnophilosophy" is "the term Paulin Hountondji used to refer to the works of those anthropologists, sociologists, ethnographers, and philosophers who present the collective world views of African peoples, their myths and folklores and folk-wisdom, as philosophy."

Clearly these professional philosophers are, for example, defining "philosophy" in terms of how intricately and rigorously a system of thought is formulated rather than in terms of the overall cohesiveness of metaphysical ideologies, etc. They're not considering the profound connotations of metaphysical principles that were known and commonly acted upon in most traditional African societies, and most indigenous societies in general, prior to colonial influence, for that matter.

Further, these scholars subscribe to, and in some instances invent, inarguably Eurocentric hierarchies.

Wiredu has a hierarchy that goes as follows: pre-literate, literate/pre-scientific, scientific. Oruka's hierarchy of thought is as follows: slave, colonial, mythological or Negritude, subjective or existential, trans-racial.

Some professional philosophers have valuable ideas. For example, Oruka's concept of "sage philosophy," which he defines as the philosophical views of traditional Africans who are regarded as wise people in their communities, priests, elders, etc. (To my knowledge no ethnophilosopher has ever failed to integrate something to the effect of Oruka's concept of sage philosophy.)

These scholars however evidently just lack skill in general in many areas of philosophy. Wiredu, for example, who is himself an Akan, claims that traditionally the Akan have no concept of Spirit, which profoundly conflicts with, for example, the works of Kwami Gyekye, who is also an Akan.

In short, the professional philosophers are evidently the least metaphysical of all black African philosophers. For this reason the term "universalist African philosophy" is very misleading.

One of the better attempts at synthesizing ethnophilosophy and professional African philosophy has been made by Messay Kebede in *Africa's Quest for a Philosophy of Decolonization* (2004).

Kebede argues for the need to integrate mythological and rational modes of evolution. But, as I will soon show, the Negritude poets did this in the first half of the twentieth century, and Kebede makes the unfortunately popular mistake of thinking that the Negritude poets did not view the traditional African psyche as having possessed/possessing rationale, that they only credited the traditional African with feeling per se.

Actually the Negritude poets had it right *per se*: African = feeling + rationale; European = rationale-feeling.

The first particularly refined metaphysic in European history was probably that of Anton Wilhelm Amo. Amo was born sometime around 1700 in Akonu, Ghana and died sometime around 1767 in Axim, Ghana. He was brought to Europe from Akonu as a child and given to the Duke of Brunswick, Anton Ulrich by The Dutch West Indies Company, who were responsible for the Dutch trade in Ghana and the Dutch missionary effort (Abraham, 1962). He was at least one of the first black people to attend a European university, possibly the first. (At least one other black person, Abram Hannibal, who was the first great modern Russian engineer, attended university in Europe around the same time that Amo did.) He taught and studied in Halle, Wittenberg and Jenna, Germany from 1727–1747. In his book *Treatise on the Art of Philosophising Soberly and Accurately* (Nwala (Ed.), 1990)—which he presented in 1737 and calls the "first fruits of [his] studies"—he argues "from existence to origin, to essence" (in the Aristotlean tradition); he understands the one-way relation between Spirit and matter, that matter is dependent on Spirit and not the reverse; he writes prodigiously about numerous eclectic subjects, like existence and non-existence, intention and will, and so on.

The system that Amo presents in *Treatise* is probably entirely more refined than, say, Hegel's or Teilhard de Chardin's, at least in some basic ways. It is way, way, way beyond, say, Kant's *The Fundamental Principles of the Metaphysic of Ethics*. (Amo wrote three works other than *Treatise* that I know of: *Dissertation on the Apatheia of the Human Mind, Disputation and the Dissertation* and *The Rights of an African in Eighteenth Century Europe* (which has, as Marilyn Sephocle puts it, "mysteriously disappeared"). But the main point that I am trying to make here is that he had an ontology, and thereby a complete metaphysic, and his epistemology was very ethics-oriented—like Plotinus', *et al*—and cohesive. (His work is also important because of the time in which he lived and the ectopic terminology that he used as a result, because of his linguistic abilities (He spoke and/or wrote roughly a dozen languages.), etc.)

Scholars like Sarvepalli Radhakrishnan (1966) and N.S.S. Raman (Deppert (Ed.), 1983) have written brilliant comparative material on Indian and European metaphysics, drawing parallels between ancient and modern Hindu systems and those of Fichte, Schelling, Hegel, etc. Amo had this type of complete metaphysic.

Amo returned to Ghana in 1751 and for the rest of his life lived in Axim where he was an Ashanti goldsmith and, according to some sources, a seer.

I believe that Frantz Fanon—the premier black psychologist, so to speak— also had the type of ontological system that I have been describing, and that his system was unlike his colleague Jean-Paul Sartre's, which was more of a continuation of Husserl's *transcendental phenomenology*, rather than a continuation of *phenomenological-existential* philosophy in the tradition of Hegel, Teilhard de Chardin, Heidegger, etc.

Hegelianism has been dramatically more popular among prominent black intellectuals and prominent intellectuals who are (or were) concerned for ethnic equality than it has been among other scholars. The first well-known psychologist to considerably embrace Hegelian phenomenology was R.D. Laing who used phenomenology in his practice of clinical psychology with overwhelming results. The whole point of phenomenological-existentialism to Laing was to demonstrate how important indigenous methods of guiding the patient on an inner journey to themselves were. Then there were the anti-technological theories of Heidegger and Lukacs' theories of social reification. Breton and the entire surrealist movement in Europe from the publication of the Second Surrealist Manifesto (1929) on were Hegelian (Balakian, 1986; Benedikt, 1974; Rosemont, 1978).

Balakian writes in *Surrealism: The Road to the Absolute* (1986), "They reintroduced to the French public a wealth of German literature." She paraphrases Breton as saying, "… despite his great antipathy for Hitler's regime, that the surrealists' confidence in German thought had not been shaken, that they considered it the most pertinent to contemporary civilization, and that they had faith in the uninterrupted cultural lineage proceeding from Hegel to Engels." Some more excerpts:

"The only mention of Hegel in the first manifesto had been an inconsequential one within a quotation from Gerard de Nerval." "… by the 1930's (…) it was the consensus of opinion that Hegel had become the pillar of their thinking. "… they were concerned with the long range problem of knowledge as well as the immediate one of expression. (...) Thinion asserted that in France the surrealists 'with the exception of a few professional philosophers, are alone in claiming derivation from Hegelian thought and in referring constantly their activities to this ideology.' He states that these ideas are of the highest importance to the surrealists and have had the power of shock on them, have led them to grasp the evolution of material and intellectual existence." "It was Hegel's stress on the superiority of the concrete over the abstract (...) particularly his definition of knowledge as the linking of thought with its object." "As Tristan Tzara said, 'It amounts to the conciliation of man in the making with the reality of the exterior world.' (...) It is not only in the deviation of the object but in the relative position of the subject and the object that Hegel serves as guide. (...) Hegel's imprint can also be noted in the philosophical significance attributed by the surrealists to the creation of the metaphor. For them it is not a mere form of speech but the crystallization of concept. (...) In Breton's understanding of the word and in the poetic and artistic interpretation given to it by the surrealist's, the ideal is not an independent concept but the result of man's mental transposition and translation of the material universe. (...) Thus both Freud and Hegel proved to be influences in the most salutary sense of the word: they pointed a direction but raised an objection strong enough to lead to subsequent originality on the part of their disciples."

What is ethnologically significant about this is that Breton, Max Ernst and others were good friends of Levi-Strauss and, a fact overlooked about as much as their Hegelianism, most of the European surrealists, including Breton, were partial to jazz.

Rosemont writes:

"The surrealists' attitude toward music underwent a significant change during and after World War II. This was not only in keeping with Breton's insistence, in the following text, on the need for a 'fundamental recasting' of the principles of music and poetry, but also in keeping with recent developments in music, most especially in American black music. Breton, who boasted that he never went to concerts, none the less made it a point to attend jazz performances during his exile in New York. And when Matta returned to Paris with recordings by Charlie Parker, Dizzie Gillespie, Bud Powell and

Thelonius Monk, bop was warmly welcomed among the surrealists, even by veterans such as the painter Victor Brauner who did an
exalted symbolic portrait titled 'Thelonius Monk'. The surrealists in
all countries increasingly have recognized in black music a fraternal
movement and a complimentary adventure. That this recognition
has not been without reciprocation is suggested by the collaboration
on Arsenal of such musicians as Cecil Taylor and Joseph Jarman."

He continues, "Many surrealists avowed an interest in jazz; the passages
on this subject scattered throughout their writings would assume a particular importance to surrealists of a later generation." He points out that Breton's
essay *Silence is Golden* is among the "least cited" of his works.

Giants of black history like Martin Luther King, Jr. and W.E.B. Du Bois singled out Hegel as their favorite philosopher. West has called Hegel "the most
adroit philosopher." Bynum has supported metaphysical aims in papers like
Research Methods in Clinical Psychospirituality (2000), drawing from Wilber's
*The Problem of Proof: A Proposal for the Verification of Sensory, Symbolic, and
Spiritual Truth Claims*. Naim Akbar, while not citing any white metaphysical
philosopher to my knowledge, has developed a good ontological and hierarchical system. Beyond this most of the most refined surrealist literature seems to
have come from Mexico, poets like Octavio Paz and Thomas Segovia, and the
West Indies (the most Africanized part of the Americas), poets like Edward
Braithwaite and Pamela Mordecai. Rarely have there been writers from Europe
or the U.S. who can compare with the best poets from Latin America, the
Caribbean or Africa. A large book could easily be devoted to a comparative
study of metaphysical elements in the literature of different ethnicities.

It is a carefully safeguarded principal in African culture that what helps one
helps all. The fact that they have historically and to this day successfully applied
this principle proves that there have traditionally been significant metaphysical
influences in African consciousness, to the extent that most African societies
can be called sociocentric. It is a relatively highly advanced mentality that considers his or her own welfare exclusively in relation to the welfare of all others
in the society.

In Africa compassion was not simply a matter of being a good samaritan.
The traditional African consciously considered the self/other duality; she considered skillfully how individuality and common laws could coexist. In Africa
neither competitiveness nor lack of self-interest were the ideal. This means that
there was, on some level, an understanding of how one faction of nature cannot

benefit from an event unless all of nature benefits from that event, a consciousness of the fact that what benefits another benefits oneself and the reverse. It was a sociocentric consciousness that had considerable worldcentric influences. Worldcentric influences were especially adhered to through indigenous priests. There were functional, spiritual hierarchies.

This is really what identifies African philosophy (from its teleological to its socio-political aspects), and its extensions branch out more rapidly than one can count them. We can view this wisdom in terms of *ngoma*, the "song-dance," in numerous parts of Africa including Zaire, Zambia, Kikongo, Angola, the Congo, Kenya and Tanzania, among others. "Song and dance are at the heart of the initiate's or celebrant's participation. The 'song-dance' [ngoma] is the product of the initiate's personal pilgrimage, and its lyrics mirror dreams, visions, as well as more mundane experiences. (…) the heart of 'doing ngoma' is the characteristic African call-and-response done so that a circle of individuals together brings out of one another the personal self of each in turn. These sessions may punctuate events of any type within the network of an order." (Janzen, 1994). On the role of rhythm in Africa Jahn writes, "To begin with, dramatic interest is not sustained by, or rather does not consist in, avoiding repetition, as in European narrative; on the contrary, the dramatic interest is born of repetition: repetition of a fact, of a gesture, of words that form a leitmotiv. But there is almost always introduction of a new element, variation of the repetition, unity in the diversity. It is this new element which underlines the dramatic advance." According to Jahn and others this applies to all expressions of African music and literature. Here is some of what Jahn writes about rhythm in Voodoo, "The rhythms change within a rhythmic system which is constructed on a polymetrical musical foundation. (…) overlaying their static accents with ecstatic emphases, producing tensions between the two. The same thing happens in all forms of African combinations of rhythm; it should probably be considered their true aim and meaning." This is dialectical. One can fake mandalic ideas with holographic theories and so on, but dialectics are hard to fake. What we have in African thought, even concerning rhythm as it pertains to sound, movement and form is an ever-inventive dialectical interplay based on a static, unifying ontology. Jahn continues, "If we add to this that every loa has its particular rhythm, that is, its specific beat, the ordering principle of this apparently disordered ecstasy becomes visible."

In Wilber's view the human race has been steadily evolving since its origins, which in Wilber's view, contrary to all anthropological and neurological evidence, is about 12,000 B.C. In my view metaphysical reasoning has been, from the beginning, about 100,000 B.C., innately natural to all humans. It is only when selfcentric individuals begin to dominate socio-politics that completely catywampus ideas about the psyche and the place of humans in nature begin to pervade the average human intelligence. To Wilber atomic energy, ozone depletion, landfill, oil-spills, clear-cutting, human cloning and innumerous other paramount problems are all understandable bi-products of the wonderful evolutionary ascent of industrialized societies. I personally do not think that spiritual evolution looks like a William Burroughs novel. To hunt for food is one thing. To war with other factions of humans is still another, but the documented history of European politics is, for the most part, one of malice. This simply does not coincide with spiritual evolution.

Suppose an individual teaches herself to read and write Mongolian Chinese in a week, then she is experiencing various neuroses, so she checks herself into a mental health facility. When the psychiatrist speaks with her most of what she says is encrypted in forms of personal, metaphorical language. The psychiatrist thinks that she is predifferentiative, that she doesn't know the difference between subjects and predicates, and so on. She is put on medication because she is thought to be psychotic. She has never even physically assaulted anyone in her life, yet the fact that she possesses an obvious linguistic virtuosity is overlooked and she is marginalized from society because her psychiatrist decides that she is mentally unfit. This is a way of trying to start from the top and dismantle the subject. What we would be doing if we were clinically integrative is starting from the bottom and building. Maybe the individual's whole problem is simply that her linguistic pursuits have never been encouraged. Nevertheless, she can be pathologized and made to feel intrinsically unhealthy.

In other words the imposition of guilt is involved here. A young man grows up in a ghetto. His sister's a prostitute. His brother was shot by a rival gang member. His father's a heroin addict. I don't think that these sociological factors are considered enough. Wilber has made brilliant statements about sociology throughout his body of work, since *The Spectrum of Consciousness*, but he does not adequately consider the influence of certain sociological conditions that he has not experienced. He has even said that we have to be wary of people who use the term the Whole, that people who use the term the All are less liable to be psychotic. His point was that we are not trying to own, we are trying to merge. Still, we compare these standards on the individual level to standards that apply on the collective level. A patient says something that doesn't sound like it came from a text book and they're pathologized and put on medication. An ethnicity brings 11 million slaves from Africa to the Americas (About forty million were taken from Africa, only about 11 million survived the conditions they were subjected to while being taken across the Atlantic.), invents gattling guns and warheads, writes a thousand libraries full of bunk history and philosophy, causes environmental and other problems at large, the Nazi regime, greed in a "religious" cloak, dissention among the Christian and Muslim ranks (In the nineteen-twenties there were over five-million members of the Ku Klux Klan in the U.S.), and all of this was supposed to have somehow been preferable to indigenous life. Good cathedrals, written language and Christianity supposedly excuse all of this, and we have supposedly, despite these unfortunate side-effects, ended up better off than we were. By these standards one could make nuclear bombs in their back yard and be a brilliant altruist.

I am not hashing industrial societies altogether, that is not my intention. What I am saying is that written language, guns, pianos and airplanes do not equal superior consciousness. The vocabulary of progressive human endeavor is entirely beyond the vocabulary of material technology. When we realize this it becomes understandable that an individual living in a thatched-roof house is as intelligent (sometimes more intelligent) as another who is developing theories in nanotechnology. If we overemphasize the extent to which material technology even potentially connotes actual spiritual consciousness we wind up with the idea that whoever is cloning humans today is far more enlightened than anyone on the planet was fifty years ago.

If, for example, written language, marked such a distinct evolutionary ascent, so distinct that it brought us from collective identification with one gender (female) to collective identification with the other (male) it would have been first produced by a faction of the human race that already had a distinctly superior spoken language. It is common knowledge among scholars that many indigenous people had some of the most efficient spoken languages in the world. The invention of written language was no more profound than the invention of the wheel. It constituted a new mode of accumulative logic, but it by no means coincided with the actual origin of accumulative logic.

In traditional Africa philosophy and religion were inseparable from each other. Aside from this African philosophy itself was monotheistic, so I must briefly address monotheism here. I will go into it in further detail in the Monotheism chapter. The idea that indigenous Africans were premonotheistic, as Wilber, Feuerstein and other prominent scholars today claim is not only contrary to what almost all insider accounts say, it is at least five dramatically distinct steps removed from what they say (van Beek and Blakely, 1994; Jahn, 1961; Parrinder, 1973; Bynum, 1999; Davidson, 1969; Magesa, 1997): first, they weren't premonotheistic; second, all African religions are generally thought by specialists on the subject to be intrinsically united; third, the same applies for exoteric African philosophy; fourth, in Africa, much like in popular Eastern traditions, i.e., Taoism, Buddhism, Hinduism, religion and philosophy are seen as inextricable from each other; fourth, linguistically, to give one good example, the Bantu language is about 3,000 years old. The dispersion of proto-Bantu root words for God, shaman, spirit, medicine and taboo have been traced throughout Africa (de Maret, 1994). And fifth, if we look more closely at the Bantu language we can see that the language itself, and how it fits into its socio-cultural context, are primarily metaphysical in the strictest sense of the word. I am not exaggerating by this. In Africa there were generally words for conscious, unconscious and spirit. These are the three components of the psyche that, as Wilber has keenly emphasized, drawing mainly from the work of Hegel, are necessary to any complete metaphysic, but they do not, in themselves connote that Africans were generally knowledgeable in the area of metaphysical philosophy.

Let us focus on Bantu linguistic ideas. There are four basic concepts in Bantu philosophy: muntu, human being; kintu, thing; hantu, place and time and kuntu, modality. As Jahn writes, "The relationship of these forces is expressed in their very names, for if we remove the determinative the stem NTU is the same for all the categories. Ntu is the universal force as such, which, however, never occurs apart from its manifestations: Muntu, Kintu, Hantu and Kuntu." We can also note that the word Bantu itself comes from the derivative ntu.

The modern trend of concentrating more on technology than psychology and religion is directly related to fact that we are living in an, as Cornel West puts it, "anti-Hegelian age." People speak about ethnic equality, but most of the same people are too engrossed in modern technology to pay attention to traditional African philosophy, which is metaphysical and psychological. It apparently never occurs to most people in industrialized societies that the Voodoo that has been given a bad name through distorted portrayals in literature, the cinema, television and the media is the same Voodoo which is the Americanized version of traditional African religion. Most people who speak about ethnic equality have negative associations with Voodoo, and it apparently never occurs to them that their ideas about Voodoo have a direct bearing on their ideas, conscious or otherwise, about black people in general. Apparently even most acculturated blacks outside of Africa have this complex.

If we can for a moment keep from being sidetracked by the relative strangeness of many African customs, possession, the idea that saliva contains psychic energy or that the white foam from a river has vitalizing powers, what we should consider first is the basic philosophical, religious and other cultural ideas which make Africans unique. What distinguishes African culture, to some extent, from every other culture of any other continent is its emphasis of esoteric principals concerning unity in diversity, and this is generally metaphysical. In no other culture is a regard for the relationship between the one and the many, the monism and the duality, as pronounced as it is in traditional African culture. We cannot find in definitive books about any other culture as common a use of words like "dialectical," "ontological," "existential," "metaphysical," "thesis, antithesis and synthesis," or terms like "determinate being" or "ontological cosmogony." This metaphysical quality (and metaphysical is probably the best word to describe it) which pervades African culture stems from African religion and philosophy contiguously. Historically it has resulted in an utterly amazing integrative ability, which has usually been unacknowledged by popular academics. Moral and ethical order, unity and individuality are all central to the traditional African mentality.

In 1986 A meeting was held by diverse scholars from four continents. This meeting led to the publication of a book titled *Religion in Africa: Experience and Expression*. It contains essays by twenty-four scholars. The purpose of the book was to present extensive accounts of a broad number of topics. Apparently the only previous book of this type was *Theoretical Explorations in African Religion* edited by van Binsbergen and Schoffeleers (1985). Blakely and van Beek write in the introduction to *Religion in Africa*, "In H. Maurier's terms, the basic experience that underlies African religious expressions, is the *je/avec* [I/with]: the antithesis of both the subject and his or her world finds a brittle but ever-to-be-regained synthesis in the sharing of identity with others. (…) Africa is a continent of relatively few people, who are continually in each other's way. In religion, Africans have repeatedly found a way out of this paradox, defining the other—opponent or partner—in such a way as to change both the other and oneself, transcending the opposition ego/alter with the notion of *relatio*, a creative synthesis that is at the heart of both African religious experience and its expression."

If this is what insider and other definitive accounts of African culture almost unanimously say, one would think that this virtuosity would be reflected in modern black academics. It is, and this is where we return to the historical patterns of the appearance of phenomenology that Wilber has overlooked. I single out Wilber because he is the only living author of psychology who has a firm understanding of metaphysics and because, really, he has presented a great overview of the evolution of white consciousness, barring a few significant mistakes, but he has not integrated the cosmological views of indigenous people, least of all Africans. While I am strongly opposed to his work on many levels, much of what I write can be seen as ethnological supplements to his work. We use many of the same terms: *mandalic consciousness, supernal philosophy, eros* and *thanatos, reductionism, elevationism*, and several others.

The components of any complete metaphysic are, as I have stated, sensory, symbolic and spirit. As I have also stated the first two can be either material or nonmaterial (spirit). Wilber has not, in my opinion, emphasized this fact enough, and this corresponds to why he does not understand African philosophy or, more specifically, the phenomenological aspects of it. I call this mode of addressing the sensory and symbolic aspects of the psyche the semi-materialistic mode.

In Papua New Guinea philosophy has resembled, as Goldman, Duffield and Ballard have noted, Heraclitean logic (Goldman and Ballard, 1998). As they have also noted, however, whereas in Heraclitean thought "the human subject is faced with the natural inevitablity of the universe, a reality that is quite unresponsive to human intervention or agency," in the traditional philosophy of the Huli and Ipili, "contrary to the implied inability of individuals to effect outcomes [they are conscious of] transformation and change as being mediated through the processes of ritual and myth." This is the consensus among all definitive texts on traditional African philosophy, whether they be philosophical or by modern black psychologists. This fact has been an underlying theme of anthologies on nonindustrial cultures like *Fluid Ontologies* (1998) and *Religion in Africa* (1994). It has also been emphasized in works by Jahn (1961), Herskovits (1958), Parrinder (1951), Magesa (1997), Davidson (1969), et al. To give two examples from *Fluid Ontologies*, in the afore mentioned essay, *Fire and Water: Fluid Ontologies in Melanesian Myth*, by Goldman, Duffield and Ballard a comparison is made between Hegelian philosophy and Huli and Ipili cosmology. In another essay from the same anthology, *Hand, Voice and Myth in Papua New Guinea*, by Weiner, explicit comparisons are made between Heideggerian philosophy and Huli cosmology. The main theme of the book, however, though references are not made to white phenomenologists in every essay, is the fifth chakra philosophy of the Huli. There were eight contributors to *Fluid Ontologies*. But the same theme runs through *Religion in Africa*, which contains essays from twenty-four authors. Really, Hegelian phenomenology is a sort of Heraclitean static philosophy combined with an understanding of the means by which humans can effect nature (including oneself) through a dynamic process. There are systems, namely, at the upper fourth chakra, that are similar to complete metaphysics, but lack an ontological basis and therefore do not constitute complete metaphysics. As I have stated, examples of this are

Jung, Socrates, Leibniz and Plotinus. So, we run into the challenge of decipher-ing upper fourth chakra systems from authentic fifth chakra (metaphysical) systems. Fifth chakra individuals include Hegel, Heidegger, Gadamer, Lukacs, Laing, Paz, Einstein and Wilber.

Perhaps the most identifiable difference between upper fourth chakra sys-tems and fifth chakra systems is that in the former genuine ontological means of mandalic consciousness are substituted by other means, such as Leibniz's relation between "symbols and things" or Jung's collective unconscious. These are ways of explicating mandalic consciousness, but they are not as functional as ontological means employed at the fifth chakra. In other words, systems based on any of the former means can only be made completely cohesive through fifth chakra means.

The prime commonality between complete metaphysics and systems that are merely influenced considerably by mandalic consciousness is that they both deal, to some functional extent, with the relation between matter and spirit. To simply concede that both matter and spirit exist and that there is a rela-tion between the two is to have a degree of mandalic (metaphysical) conscious-ness. The reason a complete metaphysic is complete is that its epistemological aspect has, what is intrinsically, a sort of (mandalic) all-access pass, namely, an authentic ontological basis.

This all-access pass is non-egoic, eros. Hegelian dialectics shows the syn-thesis of ego and non-ego. It shows that being and non-being are intrinsically unified variables of the same holonic substance. Hegelian dialectics does not come from the sensory or symbolic components per se, it comes through them. This does not insure that a fifth chakra individual's use of it will not be limited by sociological, familial or other similar influences. Thus the fifth chakra indi-vidual, since she is still egoic and thus libidinous (I will explain this further in chapter two), is prone to biases that would prevent her from understanding certain areas of mandalic reasoning. The ego exists to the extent that mandalic influences are absent.

When we look at this aspect of metaphysics explicitly its numerous more laconic possible expressions become apparent, and these types of expressions occur throughout ancient African cosmology.

Canty writes, "Akbar, like many Africentric psychologists, identifies three components of the African personality: the physical, mental and spiritual. The physical is the initial drive, tending to survival needs. The mental is the inquiry state where one attains knowledge of oneself and one's world. Lastly, the spiri-tual regulates the other two facets of the personality by giving them a moral conscience."

However, when we distinguish the "personality" from the psyche we see that according to the afore mentioned model (which is also becoming increasingly subscribed to in popular psychology) we are able to divide the psyche into three basic components—consciousness (subjective), the unconscious (relatively objective) and spirit (purely objective).

In traditional Akan psychology the dichotomy is roughly as follows: *sunsum* = consciousness; *mogya* = the unconscious and *kra* = spirit.

The Yoruba model goes, roughly: *ara* = the corporeal body; *emi* = consciousness and the unconscious; *ori* = spirit.

Prominent members of the National Association of Black Psychologists (NABP) have done an enormous amount of innovative work in many areas. Some of these areas are melanin research, the ethnology of IQ tests, research on ethnic preferences in children, and, of course, anthropology and archeology. Unfortunately most members of the NABP, including most of its prominent members, have not produced particularly great metaphysics. The one exception is Naim Akbar. Aside from this there is an exceptional sense of sociological responsibility among black psychologists. They also usually employ systems that functionally incorporate premandalic dialectics, self-knowledge, order, integration of the spiritual-intuitive and the rational-scientific, hermeneutics, and identifications of the physical, mental and spiritual spheres of the psyche-soma. There are numerous other profound qualities of contemporary psychology by blacks as well. One example is that the principle of consubstantiation (sometimes expressed ontologically) is central to most psychological systems by blacks. This as I have said, is a quality that is more pronounced in traditional Africa than anywhere else. It is also contiguous with the idea adopted by many black psychologists of European materialism, Asian spiritualism and African personalism (Asante, 1987). Unfortunately this latter model, originally proposed by Molefi Kete Asante, is usually associated by its subscribers with a view of the African concept of time as strictly "circular" and the European concept as strictly "linear". This, as I have implicitly stated, is a popular misconception, since anyone who can read a calendar thinks (at least partially) linearly. In traditional Africa, as in most indigenous cultures (pan-geographically), there was usually something of a balance between concepts of linear and circular (or cyclic and accumulative) time. And, again, a certain understanding of metaphysics is necessary to any concept of how cyclic and accumulative time coexist. So, lack of metaphysical understanding leads to the implicit promulgation that nonindustrial cultures do not understand calendars.

Appropriately, these psychologists generally trace their fundamental theories back to Africa. More precisely they trace them back to dynastic Egypt, about 3500 B.C., or, often, earlier Ethiopia or predynastic Egypt. The systems that they have formulated are generally remarkably similar to each other, and they have apparently formulated these systems, basically, independently of each other. Humanism, in the refined sense, is central to many of their theories. They usually point out Aristotle's four levels of causation and so on. "White (1984) views the holistic, humanistic ethos described by Nobles (1972) and Mbiti (1970) as the principle feature of African psychology. There appears to be a definite correspondence between the African ethos and the Afro-American worldview in terms of the focus on emotional vitality, interdependence, collective survival, the oral tradition, perception of time, harmonious blending, and the role of the elderly." (Parham, White and Ajamu, 1999). Their work is generally both noetic and somatic. There is much to be said in terms of the metaphysical contributions of the NABP. The best metaphysical philosopher among them is probably Akbar.

Most black psychologists use terms like ontology and dialectics generously, but many of them, i.e., Edward Bruce Bynum and Linda James Myers, fall prey to preontological systems like the holographic paradigm. Among the work that they have produced, the most catalytic text by a single author is possibly Bynum's *The African Unconscious*. Here is an excerpt:

"One path, or pattern of the dance, leads into the psychospiritual union of opposites and unseen harmonies beyond intellectual or rational understanding and into deep identification with the dark and yet luminous transcendental source of revelation. The other path tends to see matter as primary, leads eventually to a philosophy of randomness and chance, the ghostly god of probability, the exhausted philosophy of existential angst and ennui. Personhood and spirit are the sisters of matter and energy. The path of materialism eventually arches toward separation from matter and nature, dissociation from self-ablating revelation and, yes, eventually the fragmentation and subtle toxicity of logical positivism."

Authors like Bynum and Myers collapse the hierarchy. They do not understand, say, the difference between holographic consciousness and mandalic consciousness. All of this shows in their work. Myers, for example, mentions holonic aspects of African philosophy, but she has no authentic understanding of holons. Bynum has attempted to equate the physical, mental and spiritual aspects of the individual with Wilber's sensory, symbolic and spirit aspects of the psyche, but he does not understand the sensory, symbolic and spirit levels. In my opinion Wilber is in many ways, though all inadvert, doing as much for our understanding of traditional African philosophy as most members of the NABP.

The lack of metaphysical skill among most members of the NABP is also evidenced in their comparisons between traditional African philosophy and, for example, popular forms of Eastern philosophy. They usually give great exoteric comparisons, but they do not address the esoteric commonalities. The esoteric commonalities (as with the traditional philosophies of virtually any culture) can only be explained phenomenologically.

The NABP also usually distorts the history of racism among white people and white academics. It does not exaggerate the history of racism among white people; rather, it shifts the focus inaccurately thereby expressing a distorted view of when, where and how racism has existed (and does exist) among white people. Racism was not as prominent among whites until after the beginning of the colonial period. Herodotus and Homer both commended the black race explicitly. Members of the NABP also often try to present white academics in general as having almost zero value. This quote from Wade Nobles (who is not even an Afrocentrist) is a good example, "Freud, though he belonged primarily to dynamic psychology, stands almost alone as representing the field of psychology." (Nobles, 1986). Nobles then goes on to relate Freud's Oedipal theory to the Orphic mystery of ancient Greece; all of this in an attempt to sum up the inadequacy of western psychology and the western psyche. Similarly distorted statements are found in the work of Myers, Azibo, Bynum and others. We can see from the excerpt from Noble's *African Psychology: Toward Its Reclamation, Reascention & Revitalization* what is happening. Black psychologists are doing the same thing to white history that most white scholars have done to black history since the beginning of European colonization. Still there is no justification for racism, either by the oppressors or the oppressed. Both sides lack ethnological resourcefulness, and this will have to be out grown if we are to understand the supernal philosophy as it pertains to the equal contributions of all ethnicities.

The NABP was founded in 1968 in response to the hegemonious conditions which blacks faced and, to an extent, in response to the opinion among many black psychologists that white scholars had not produced an adequate system of psychological study. "The Black portion of the total pool of psychology doctorates from 1920 to 1950 probably was less than 1 percent.... Of the 21,225 psychology doctorates issued between 1975 and 1981, 706 (3.33 percent) were awarded to Blacks." (Houston, 1990). From the original members of the NABP two schools formed: the "pro-black" and the "Afrocentric".

The term Afrocentric was coined by Asante in the eighties. Many individuals in the movement prefer the term Africentric. Afrocentrism as Asante defined it is not racist. In his words, "Some authors have mistaken European agitation, manifested as a rhetorical reaction to social, religious, and political repression, with African protest discourse that seeks the removal of oppression." Asante is existential but not hierarchical. He dismisses scholars like Heidegger and Levi-Strauss in favor of Sartre, whose work I am not particularly a fan of.

Afrology, in Asante's conception is a broad field involving the unification of affective, cognitive and conative theories and practices, and this is how most Afrocentrists and other black psychologists have interpreted and employed it.

The base philosophical aspect of Afrocentrism, as defined by Asante, is similar to Sartre's dialectics. Negritude, however, according to Leopold Senghor—who, with Aime Cesaire, coined the term—is directly related to Hegelian phenomenology. (Some sources say that the term Negritude was first used in Cesaire's long poem *Notebook of a Return to the Native Land*, 1939.) More precisely, Senghor locates the origins of European dialectical thought in Hegel's work and states that this method is indispensable for any thorough understanding of Negritude. In Senghor's view, however, the dialectics of Teilhard de Chardin was closer to the traditional African ideology than any other philosophical system produced by a European or philosopher of European extraction. This was his view of Teilhard de Chardin as philosopher and scientist.

This is a brilliant observation. Senghor is probably correct for numerous reasons. And there are many parallels between Teilhard de Chardin's work and Hegel's. Teilhard de Chardin's work, in my view, is much closer to Hegel's than are the works of Husserl or Rollo May. At the same time I think that a relatively small number of scholars understand the works of either Teilhard de Chardin or Hegel particularly well. Thus the commonalities between their systems have not been adequately understood often enough, and Senghor's definition of Negritude in turn has also rarely been understood. But Negritude, as Senghor defined it, is, in my opinion, brilliant.

The Afrocentric movement seems, for the most part, to have replaced the Negritude movement. I do not think that this was entirely regressive on the parts of black people. Afrocentrism is largely about rejecting the notion of any necessity to fit into white terminology or other white constructs. The Afrocentric movement has a powerful and necessary message: We are not the students of whites any more than they are our students. Also, since the word *negro*, for whatever reasons, became archaic by the eighties, the term *Afrocentrism*, in a way, makes more sense than *Negritude*. While I prefer Teilhard de Chardin to Sartre, the Afrocentric movement has, in many ways been indispensable.

Many scholars have misinterpreted Senghor's message as simply being that the European is rational while the African is emotional. In Senghor's words, "The vital force of the Negro African, his surrender to the object, is animated by reason. (...) It is not the reasoning-eye of Europe, it is the reason of the touch, better still, the reasoning-embrace, the sympathetic reason, more closely related to the Greek *logos* than to the Latin *ratio*." The black African is discursive, but he does not fix the object in order to use it for selfcentric purposes. Rather it is a discursive reasoning wherein the object is embraced ontologically, in accord with the principle of consubstantiation.

While Senghor asserts that Teilhard de Chardin's phenomenology was closer to that of traditional Africa than any other produced by a white philosopher, Teilhard de Chardin's phenomenology was in many ways more theological than philosophical in the formal sense. Senghor was correct about the similarities between Teilhard de Chardin's work and traditional Africa philosophy. Here, however, I am trying to illustrate the basic technical qualities of traditional African philosophy as they relate to historical European philosophy rather than the overall approach (emotional or otherwise) by which traditional African ideas are reached. Thus my emphasis (in this context) on the uniformity between Hegelian phenomenology and the philosophy of traditional Africa. As I have stated, Teilhard de Chardin's system and Hegel's are, in my view, particularly similar.

Senghor did cite Sartre often, but this was largely because Sartre sort of had a hand in the Negritude movement. For example, Sartre wrote the preface, titled *Black Orpheus*, for Senghor's *Anthologie de la Nouvelle Poesie Negre et Mangache* and was on the advisory board for the journal *Présence Africaine*.

The Akan philosopher Kwame Gyekye (1997) identifies two types of universalism: essential and contingent. Though the manner in which Hegel expressed his ideas was endemic to Europe (contingent universalism) the underlying messages were of an essential universal nature.

Both Senghor and Cesaire were surrealist poets. Senghor was also President of his native Senegal from 1960–1980, and Cesaire was a Martinican who served as mayor of Fort-de-France (Martinique's capital) for many years and as a deputy in the French National Assembly.

On the whole, black psychologists are not only closer to a complete metaphysic, they are consistently closer, and they consistently trace their systems (which are generally similar to each other's) to ancient Africa.

White hegemony is primarily the result of two historical events: 1) slavery and 2) the expansion of technology. I do not believe that whites have always been the spiritually inferior ethnicity. Racism among whites did not begin to expand considerably until the two afore mentioned events happened. Racism in white texts was propagated and perpetuated in congruence with the original European conquests of nonindustrial people in general and was issued further in an attempt to make the enslavement of blacks in the Americas and Europe appear justified. Many scholars, especially those who are people of color, are thoroughly aware of this fact. The technology issue, on the other hand, has gone relatively overlooked in its full connotations. When whites began to mass produce bicycles and cars Africa is where the rubber for the tires came from. The human faculty of narcissism is strong. With technological developments arose the idea that material technology equals superior intelligence. As technology has expanded historically, and continues to this day, so has the narcissistic misconception associated with it. I will add here (and I will go into detail about this in the third chapter) that blacks have contributed nearly as much to the fields of science and medicine, despite their circumstances, as whites have. "White man's medicine," as Wilber calls it, is not in fact white anyone's medicine. Blacks have made paramount contributions to both technology and medicine from the earliest period, given the manifold evolutionary accomplishments of the ancient Egyptians in fields from mathematics and medicine to literature and architecture, which we know about from their own accounts, from those of the ancient Greeks and from the vital works of scholars like Charles Finch, Theophile Obenga, Bynum, Davidson and many others.

Wilber writes, "At even the earliest point that historical reality was discovered, it was infected with the egotistical notion that history was, first and foremost, a chronicle of the egos accomplishments and heroic feats. The first recorded histories were, as we saw, tales of egoic (kingly) victories and triumphs and daring feats, usually in battle, always boastful." He then continues, "But the actual truth concealed in the new mode of historical time was the truth that consciousness is our destiny and awakening our fate; the truth that the world is indeed going somewhere, meaningfully: it is going toward Atman." But the bicameral mind never existed. Most of what has been written in history has been written by third chakra individuals. It was the nonindustrial people, the ones who avoided the invention of the gattling gun and the release of atomic energy, smoke stacks and landfill, who were more evolved. In time most people blended into industrial societies as well as they could or enough to derive some sort of comfort from the circumstances. White people simply blended in better. Today over five-thousand distinct indigenous cultures resist industrialization.

When I say that most people blended into industrial societies I am including people on whom industrial acculturation was forced.

The European dissociation was not the bi-product of any transformation. Europe has made great accomplishments since the beginning of history. But none of these accomplishments were expressions of a collective transformation either. As everyone knows, most of the greatest artists in documented history have lived in poverty. Wilber has the European dissociation basically right except that it did not coincide with any collective European transformation. The written word was nothing other than a translation of the spoken word. Nano-technology is nothing other than a translation of the wheel.

Akbar writes, "The pervasive African conception is that man is essentially spirit. Therefore survival of the spirit represents the ultimate survival of the human being. (…) [The hunger of the spirit] is actually a metaphysical hunger—a hunger for the infinite. The body hungers for finite ingredients-physical food, sensual experience, physical reproduction, etc. The mind hungers for knowledge, enlightenment, order, communication." Of his system he writes, "Though it describes the human being as manifesting life on several planes—physical, mental, and spiritual—it also describes the unity of those strivings."

Akbar is a leading theorist of black psychology and a former President of the NABP, but most systems by modern black psychologists are remarkably similar to his. They successfully map out relations between the finite and the infinite, between the conscious, the unconscious and the spirit. In some ways they do this better than the best white authors of psychology, including Wilber and Nelson. As Phillips writes, "people-to-people orientation is primary to the Afrocentric value system." This is also stated by Myers, "Self-knowledge being the basis of all knowledge, the unconditional positive regard for the natural order must begin within and be generated outwardly, manifesting at a critical point in terms of interpersonal relations among people." So, the task is to identify metaphysical from quasi-metaphysical systems. And here we are doing this in regard to traditional African philosophy and modern psychology by black authors. Most black authors of psychology today identify three components of the psyche: physical, mental and spiritual. These are the terms that they usually use. These components of the psyche can be treated either metaphysically (equated to Wilber's sensory, symbolic and spirit components, explicitly or otherwise) or they can be treated quasi-metaphysically, (depth psychology, holistic theory and so forth). Either way most black psychologists identify these three levels, and they draw functional distinctions between each of them. A concern for order, the balance between spiritual intuition and rational science and awareness of both "circular" and "linear" time has been extensively stated in these works.

The European dissociation was partly a dissociation of the importance of healthy relationships between people. This is reflected in the best psychology texts by white authors even today. Black psychologists rarely have this shortcoming. This quality is emphasized in all definitive texts on African culture, i.e., Parrinder, Jahn, Herskovits, Magesa, et al., as well as all prominent psychology texts by black authors. This corresponds to a more teleological and somatic world view, and to a world view that is, in my opinion, much more socio-politically realistic. Wilber, for example, states correctly that hatha yoga exemplifies somatic-existentialism, but in his terminology mind is higher than nature. Mind is not higher than nature. Mind is an inextricable part of nature. The symbolic level is not higher than the sensory level, and the human psyche, especially if it is to be viewed as one with the human soma, is not entirely above matter. The spirit integrates and transcends matter and both the sensory and symbolic components of the psyche can express spirit, but this does not warrant a system in which humans are considered to be above nature per se. Holons too can be at various hierarchal stages of evolution, but it is not so much where we are as it is the direction in which we are moving. In my view using a term as hermeneutically broad as *mind* to express something beyond nature tends to lead to the dissociation of nature. In turn this produces irrational ideas about the value of material technology and so forth. Basically, the reason that I disagree with his use of the term mind is that often people use their minds in ways that are subhuman. Human cloning is an example, and here we are referring to the epitome of material technology. But, of course, Wilber's use of the term is geared to support his Eurocentric theory of the solar logos. This is not only absurd because of the manifold uses of sun, light, sky and other celestial symbolism in nonindustrial mythologies and so forth, but also because people in industrial societies even today are hardly more individualistic than people in nonindustrial societies, nor are individualism or integrity more supported in industrial societies.

The emphasis on interpersonal relationships, as particularly expressed in definitive texts pertaining to Africa is also similar to the "antipsychiatry" of Laing. Laing rejected the term antipsychiatry. The point, however, is that Laing largely believed that people should be supported in the process of discovering themselves in the face of socio-political adversity. "For example, human purpose, (the distortion of which is the root of almost all human mal-functioning short of biological or chemical based maladies) and the 'meaningfulness' of one's action are revealed in the awareness of one's intent and will. Similarly, a sense of as collective or extended (i.e., *pars pro toto*), the comprehension and respect of the sameness of self and others; the interdependence and synthesis of human beings, etc. all emerge from and are dependent upon the African ontological principle of consubstantiation." (Nobles, 1986). Presently we have in industrial societies the negation of these principles. A patient walks into a mental institute. The doctor asks her if she is hearing voices, and if the patient does not speak like a textbook they are often forced to take medication.

The hierarchy, up to the fifth chakra (I will explain this in more detail in the second chapter) exists as Wilber states, aside from his Eurocentrism, but the neuroses latent among these levels cannot be underestimated in relation to socio-political circumstances. As Nelson states most people in industrial societies are at the third chakra. This makes it particularly difficult for individuals who are beyond this, especially if they are at the fifth chakra, to maintain an attunement to themselves. Often they need clinical help, and usually it is the sort of help described by Laing and most black psychologists rather than medication which generally is not supplemented by the type of understanding necessary to a genuine healing process. We are emphasizing the principle of consubstantiation as it applies to all levels of the hierarchy.

The word existential in phenomenological-existential philosophy epitomically connotes the fact that there must be healthy relations between physical beings. If this was not necessary we would not be physical beings. The socio-political orchestration of genuinely healthy relations between people and between people and nature in itself connotes a profound degree of fifth chakra influence because it requires an understanding (or, at least, an intuition on some level) of the ontological relation between matter and spirit (metaphysics). In a sense, ones regard for the importance of healthy relations between physical beings defines their phenomenological capacity. The most refined application of this ethos lapses into the type of panentheism that we find in most indigenous cultures. Indigenous, semiotic expressions of this are generally mistaken by Wilber to be predifferentiative nature amalgamations. This is not only a mistake on his part, it is the result of his own dissociation of his ontological relation to the rest of nature. In Wilber's hierarchy there is the subconscious, the selfconsious and the superconscious, in that order, or nature, mind and spirit. If we view the hierarchy this way then mental expressions, "distorted" or otherwise are above natural expressions. This is the exact mistake that has led to the underestimation of indigenous cultures. It is not optimally sympathetic with nature. Wilber, in fact, ascribes panentheism to his subtle level (level six), which does not exist.

Akbar, in his book *Natural Psychology and Human Transformation*, has hierarchically described what seem to be chakras three through five. He has done this in reference to the nafs of the Quran and using the transformation of the butterfly as a metaphor. He has also helped to restore the ancient indigenous understanding that "All matter is composed of the four elements of earth, fire, air and water."

The mind transcends nature only to the extent that ones mental expressions come from spirit. Even this depends on the context, since nature in its totality is transholonic.

Jahn writes, "Death as destroyer is a Western conception. We may therefore risk the assertion that the philosophical system we have been describing is valid not only for the Bantu and the Dogon and the Bambara, and not only for Africa, but for African culture in general, both traditional and modern. And we can take it as a touchstone in our further investigations, when we want to know how far African culture extends, what works of art, poems and novels belong to it and what do not."

In ancient Africa magara was rightly considered the most valuable "currency." They looked at magara on the level of interaction between the living and the dead. They considered these interactions in terms of their conscious and unconscious existence. This is another way of illustrating the three aspects of the psyche, sensory, symbolic and spirit in African philosophy and religion. Jahn writes, "'The sheep was at Kapundwe's house, that is, under his life influence. Everything that happened to the sheep, for good or ill, can, according to the Bantu conception, be ascribed to the life influence, whether conscious or unconscious.' Kapundwe gave what according to the European view was such an enormous compensation because the man from Busangu said: 'The loss of my sheep pains me, it gives me sorrow.' After the reparation by one sheep he was still suffering. Only after he had had three sheep and a hundred francs could he forget his sorrow, and feel himself once more a living, happy man, only then was his life force, his magara, restored."

The pervading metaphysical qualities of Latin American, Caribbean and African literature—i.e., in the works of Marco Antonio Montes De Oca, Thomas Segovia, Jose Emilio Pacheco, Jose Lezama Lima, Pablo Neruda, Edward Braithwaite, Derek Walcott, Niyi Osundare, Jared Angira, Tchicaya U Tam'si, etc.—are rooted in traditional regards for death. (Here I am not trying to downplay the fact that a notable amount of wonderful surrealist poetry, etc. has been coming out of even contemporary Europe—i.e., the works of poets from the Czech Republic like Tomaz Salamun, and so on.) In African and other indigenous traditions death was viewed existentially, but it was not viewed as simply an end; rather it was viewed as a transition, after which the "living" could remain in contact with the spirit of the departed. The life force (or magara) of the deceased did not cease to be. It merely ceased to be embodied on the earthly plane. Africans and other indigenous people keenly understood this distinction, and it is expressed much easier in most African languages than it is in most European languages, including English.

There is a difference between not being on the earthly plain and not having magara. More esoterically there is an important difference between, say, mental and non-material. When we consider the sensory (unconscious, emotion) and symbolic (conscious) levels (the two that are potentially material) what we find is that emotions can be either spiritual or material and that the same applies for thoughts. In African philosophy everything is geared toward the simultaneous exaltation of the individual (or self) and the collective. It is a philosophy of interaction, and it is through this interaction, which is generally meticulously structured, that the life force grows for the individual, the society and all of nature.

Human metaphysical consciousness, both ontological and pre-ontological, assumably originated in ancient Africa. And it probably, for all we can tell about the history and prehistory of basic senses of temporality, etc., originated at least as early as cir. 50,000 B.C. It may have originated tens of thousands of years prior to the emergence of verbal language. Because of this mainstream and popular scholars will discover and more skillfully define historical threads of African, European, Indian, Asian, etc. metaphysical thought as they refer back to how ancient people—including Socrates, Plotinus, *et al.*—regarded the relation between empirical and metaphysical reasoning.

While ritual and what Asante calls "palliative" unifying processes in general were/are, of course, vital aspects of traditional African culture, the wide-spread simultaneous exaltation of feeling and dissociation of reason (The popular view that critical thinking somehow automatically negates action, et al.) among apparently all but the minutest percent of supposedly progressive, non-lumpen proletariat people in the First World goes hand-in-hand with exoticism, etc.

In Africa, traditionally, truth is sought by priests, elders and the people, but it is sought—in regard to psychology, cosmology, socio-politics, taxonomy, etc.—using modes of sense and thought that are not apprehensive in certain ways that European modes, by and large, pervasively are. Priests in most traditional African societies, like their nearest equivalents in traditional China, India, etc., viewed religion as integrating and transcending philosophy. While they did differentiate and think hierarchically and linearly (I realize that a lot of people have a difficult time imagining an indigenous African reading a calendar.), as Senghor explains, their reasoning was "more closely related to the Greek *logos* than to the Latin *ratio*."

CHAPTER TWO

Monotheism

Monotheism did not originate in conjunction with the dawn of Christianity. Monotheism is constituted by the original concept of something greater than ourselves which created all of nature. This was basic to most original cultures. It was not a European or Indo-European invention. Whether or not various monotheistic cultures included pantheons does not reflect on their abilities to understand monotheism or their abilities to differentiate the roles of the genders as they pertain to religion. Polytheism is derived from different sources. By worshipping the one supreme God we are worshipping the source of all divine principles. In a region where droughts are latent, however, one might pray to a rain god. If there are complex decisions to be made one might pray to a god of travel, to guide them on the right path. Catholics pray to Saint Christopher for this purpose. So, neither Europeans nor Indo-Europeans were religiously superior to most indigenous people. If one goes with the Christian faith, it took a great shaman to convert Europeans to a more refined form of monotheism than what they had. After this they had a more distinct form of monotheism. They still did not have panentheism, nor did they regard spiritual issues rationally (metaphysics). Indigenous Europeans, prior to the European dissociation and regression were consubstantiative; they regarded the *other* the way all indigenous people, collectively, did prior to colonial influence. Most indigenous people already had panentheism and other modes of metaphysical thought that they adhered to through their priests. Somehow a number of the most prominent transpersonal psychologists today have managed to dismiss this as being congruent with pre-rationalism.

Monotheism is simply the belief in no more than a single creator. Christianity is as monopantheonistic as most monopantheonisms. The angels, really, are nothing other than deities. There were four archangels in the Hebrew Bible. Ironically, when African slaves were brought to the Americas they equated Catholic Saints with their deities. They were monotheistic, but they built temples and altars to ancestors and other divinities and virtually none to the

Supreme Being. We see this and other patterns among indigenous people pan-geographically.

These supposed pre-monotheists, world-wide, were not only monotheistic, they were largely panentheistic, meaning that they viewed God as being in all of nature and yet transcending nature. Traced syllogistically, this view is holonic and metaphysical. Native North Americans worship the Creation, as in "Unity under the Creation." In the popular Native American view there never was a descent from Eden. In their view all is simply part of the same web of life. Wilber would argue that this is pre-rational, I say it is rational. It is a basic tenet of the supernal philosophy that one should not act for oneself without having an equal concern for the well being of the rest of the world. With the creation we have the monad, the unity of all of nature (the relative universe, or what Wilber might call the Great Holon), and Native Americans worship this monad. Yet something created it because it is called the Creation. Here we have a perfectly sophisticated religious view. A monad, which is like the whole of the shadows in Plato's cave, and something which created the monad, which is like the light at the end of Plato's cave. Perfectly metaphysical. This does not explicitly describe the metaphysical anatomy and functions of the psyche, but it does involve the relation between the physical and the spiritual planes, which is metaphysical. This is essentially what is described in Hinduism. Different versions of this paradigm are widespread throughout the continents. It should not be held against anyone if they cannot help but have a spiritual reverence for, say, trees, wind or the sun. If people thought of an active volcano as a god, or of a giant tree as a god it was because these aspects of nature are more awesome than any empirical invention could ever be. Only in rare cases did this mean that they were not monotheistic. Holonically (thus in terms of the supernal philosophy as well) everything in the material world embodies its own divine principle. Everything is a law of nature on some level, whether this level has been brought to light at any given time or not. Thereby, rationally, the most basic way to view any divine entity who is not the Supreme is in terms of it being a unique law of nature. A law of nature because, intrinsically, according to esoteric holonic theory that's what bestows divine order, these potentially infinite laws of nature, which are factions of the Divine Oneness. Angels in Christianity are divine entities. They are, according to holonic theory, laws of nature. The same is true for all pantheons. Christians regarded a pantheon. They didn't call it a pantheon. They simply called this pantheon angels, saints and archangels. But they served the same theoretical function as any pantheon. Until about a decade ago one could not normally tell a Christian that God lives in a tree. The

Christian would have thought you were a witch. Historically Christians have not interpreted the Bible metaphysically, panentheistically or even rationally.

In the Bible there is the serpent from the Garden of Eden. Moses took up the asp. There is the lion and the lamb. There are plenty of animal metaphors in the Bible. Other religions also have animal metaphors. But they are metaphors. Unlike common Christians throughout the historical past, people from other cultures understood that animal metaphors were metaphors.

Europeans tend to be rigid-minded to the point of being unable to discern figurative speech from literal, mechanical speech. This is, no doubt, why Shakespearean poetry is full of spoon-fed metaphors compared to most non-European poetry. (A subject I will explain in detail in chapter four.) There was Aesope. There is the wolf in Little Red Riding Hood. There is "the cat and the fiddle," "the cow [who] jumped over the moon," and plenty of other examples of European animal metaphors. Native Americans never thought that Grandmother Spider was a literal spider. It was Europeans who took the animal archetypes of these indigenous religions literally, and who continue to do this. These indigenous people were entirely more adept at understanding metaphors. This is why, when modern anthropologists discovered the Tasaday—who live in a rainforest in the Philippines with only the simplest tools—they were dumbfounded by the fact that the Tasaday were able to use metaphorical and literal language interchangeably. The Tasaday live mostly in caves to this day. They have no known word for war. They are not even particularly agricultural. They only knew of one clearing when they were discovered, and they avoided it. To the anthropologists their understanding of metaphors was an amazing feat.

In Persia, for example, in 1900 B.C. a form of monotheism was established. This is the sort of thing that is overemphasized by Eurocentric scholars.

In Wilber's theory everything is cut and dry in terms of equations between different forms of industrial monotheism as they manifested on the human, evolutionary scale. He would argue vehemently against this, but it's true. He pays attention to imaginary neurological factors and so forth, which have no actual grounding in neurology. According to him monotheism is originally exclusively patriarchal. The Egyptians were able to write what even he acknowledges was exquisite metaphysics, but they weren't monotheistic. Even Egyptologists, who are among the most hard-headed of scientists, acknowledge the monotheism of dynastic Egyptians. If geologists and paleoclimatologists popularly argue with Egyptologists about the date of the origin of the Sphinx, Egyptologists simply stick to their story despite overwhelming evidence by specialists in other fields.

To illustrate the diversity and complexity that Wilber has overlooked among forms of monotheism at large, some ancient, hundreds of others being new, I will give one example: Shintoism.

Shintoism originated about 2,500–3,000 B.C. It's hierarchy of divinities is, at the top, comprised of the Supreme Being, then a male and female who created the world, then two goddesses and one god. This god, in Shinto mythology, is considered to have been the malevolent force among the three divine siblings. This, combined with the fact that he was outnumbered by two sisters who happen to be the sun goddess and the moon goddess, makes Shintoism primarily a matriarchal religion. Also, in Shintoism the worship of other divinities, many of whom are associated with nature and various ideological principles, and of ancestors, who, as in traditional Africa, can become divinities, is prevalent. In fact, as in traditional Africa, thousands of shrines are dedicated to these manifold divinities and ancestors.

Shintoism is probably as similar to ancient African religion as any other religion, indigenous or otherwise. This is not only because of the extent to which thousands of divinities and ancestors are worshipped and because of certain pronounced commonalities between Shinto and pan-African creation myths. Traditional Shinto philosophy, including socio-political ideas, is largely similar to traditional African philosophy as well.

Sources generally say that most Japanese are both Shinto and Buddhist. By referring to Shinto alone we can see many elements of the complex historical diversity among forms of religion pan-geographically. Zen Buddhism, which Wilber says has "produced the most masters", originated in Japan, though it was derived from Chinese Taoism. Zen, like all popular forms of Buddhism, is thoroughly patriarchal. Wilber does not explain how the popularity of Shintoism coincides to this day with the popularity of Zen Buddhism in Japan. The Japanese, like the Chinese, have, in many areas, competed with the United States and other historical "super powers" in terms of technological developments.

How do the Japanese, who epitomize patriarchy and technology and who produced Zen Buddhism adhere to a religion like Shintoism, which is both thoroughly engrained in Japanese culture and pronouncedly similar to various forms of indigenous religion, especially African?

This is only one way of addressing the issue. Then we have profoundly contrasting views of morality among different types of monotheism. In Japan suicide, or seppuku, has been traditionally considered ethical under certain conditions. White cultures historically have had the opposite view of suicide. All of this reflects the actual diversity of otherwise comparable and more or less equal religions, which is far more eclectic than Wilber chooses to recognize. We have to consider this when we investigate any religion, including indigenous African religions, which have unjustly had a mass stigmatism projected on them.

Most indigenous cultures were monotheists, like Christians. They believed in one Creator, from which everything in the material universe originated and to which everything in the material universe eventually returns. They also usually had pantheons. These were composed of angels, like the Christian pantheon. It is a popular myth that indigenous cultures did not have their own words for the Supreme Being (Jahn, 1961; Davidson, 1969; Parrinder, 1973; Magesa, 1997; Lugira, 1999; Blakely, 1994).

In Voodoo the Supreme Being is called Olorun. Voodoo dolls are part of Holly Wood. Voodoo is generally a positive religion. When it adopted elements of Catholicism, it was Catholicism that was integrated into Voodoo, not the reverse. In Voodoo animals are often sacrificed and the person who becomes possessed by the loa often drinks the blood of the sacrifice. This can be compared to the eucharist in Catholicism.

In traditional Africa the blood is often offered to the gods and/or ancestors. In other cultures it is simply spilled without any regard for the animal's spiritual well-being. In third world countries some people live off of animal blood. In traditional African religion animals are sacrificed in humane ways and as a sincere gesture of the participants' reverence for divinities and ancestors which help them maintain moral and ethical order within their societies.

Neither in indigenous nor in transplanted forms of African religion do ceremonies typically involve any form of orgiastic energy, as is commonly thought by outsiders. The only way most industrialized people can conceive of the use of animal blood in a religious ritual is in a negative manner. This is a gross projection. This misconception of traditional African religion has nothing to do with African religion itself. It is solely the product of the general mentalities of industrialized people.

Jahn describes relations between Voodoo and Santeria, how similar they are, that they come from "neighboring and friendly sects of the same religion," that santeria comes from the Ife. Certain words are virtually intact. The priest in santeria, for example, is called babalao after the Ife babalawo. He also points out complex differences, "in Africa the masks are clearly divided into bazimu— and bazima—masks but in Cuba the distinction is obscured."

Ekue means death. In the Nanigo cult of Cuba they call him the "Great Mystery." Jahn writes that "since the absolute transcends all human understanding, no temples are built to Olorun either in Yorubaland or in Cuba, and no sacrifices made to him." He also writes, however, that at the very beginning of the Nanigo ceremony the initiate sacrifices "the blood of a cock to the 'Great Mystery', to Ekue." He writes of Santeria, "just as in Voodoo, he becomes the orisha ... We can see this clearly if we compare the Santeria with Naniguismo."

He describes the Nanigo ceremony as theatrical. A male sheep and at least two chickens are sacrificed, people drink blood, and participants chase each other around a silk-cotton tree in a theatrical manner.

One of the greatest challenges for any writer concerned with judicial interpretations of the comparative, historical development of African and European cultures is balancing the interface between what is basically identical and what is profoundly different between the two subjects. Bias comes from not viewing comparisons from a genuinely worldcentric view. Where there are significant differences between two subjects one tends to favor the subject that she or he is more familiar with.

It takes particular foresight to decipher how absolute differences can reflect absolute samenesses. By the same right it takes intuition to perceive how absolute samenesses can reflect absolute differences. Mindfulness of these two objective elements of comparative study is lacking in most existing texts on African and other indigenous cultures. We can add to the afore mentioned factors, which we can view as a thesis and antithesis, in either order, the fact that the two are often combined in innumerous extremely intricate ways. The combination of the two potentially forms a synthesis. This synthesis, when it occurs, constitutes invariably the reification of natural order into social order (Lukacs, 1971).

This can manifest verbally (not necessarily through the written word), architecturally, agriculturally, so on. It can manifest in any natural area of human endeavor, and all of these expressions of natural order, where they appear, reveal nothing less than an understanding of natural order on some sovereign socio-political level.

So, we're talking about the assessment of what, for example, constitutes an expression of a conscious regard for natural order in architecture. Already the factors are out of hand by modern, industrialized, psychological standards.

Congruently, when a society thinks this way or reveres individuals who do what is constituted is a collective fourth or fifth chakra consciousness. In most cases I think that nonindustrial societies were primarily at the fourth chakra and that the shamans and priests that they held in highest regard were usually fifth chakra or higher. Collectively I think that most nonindustrial cultures were at the fourth chakra. Here I am basically using the chakra system described in John Nelson's *Healing the Split*. Here at the basic psychological level we can begin to assess what differences and similarities there are between industrial and nonindustrial cultures. We can look at empirical developments, but the only way to translate the reasons for the existence or nonexistence of any empirical development in any given society is by assimilating the purpose of that presence or absence as members of the respective society saw it in the context of their cosmological, philosophical, psychological and religious views. In short, we must consider empirical developments in the context of any metaphysical and/or religious cultural elements that we can derive.

On one hand we have this network of psychological, metaphysical factors to consider with, at their center, the reification of natural order into social order. One cannot really reach a verdict about the overall consciousness of a society based only on empirical traits. The empirical traits cannot be overlooked, but to understand what they reveal about a society one must consider them adequately in their objective socio-psychological contexts.

The original Roman conquest of North Africa began in the 1100s. Between the seventeenth and nineteenth centuries 11 million people from west and central Africa would be brought to the Americas as slaves. The number of people exterminated during the African holocaust could be reasonably estimated to be around 200 million. This is about 34 times the amount of Jews executed during World War II. It was mostly the British who were responsible for this unprecedented atrocity, although the Portugese had a large part in the slave trade originally and, of course, Muslims, whose colonialism is very commonly glossed over even by prominent Africanist scholars today, conquered all of Mediterranean Africa in the seventh century (the century Islam was founded) and whatnot. Today, *despite the very wide-spread liberalism at large*, those who are above the poverty level, at least throughout the western hemisphere, by and large, still think that Europeans and people of European extraction (i.e., those from North America and the Arabian Peninsula) unified the indigenous societies that they colonized, when it could not be more obvious that they divided them. This is a vital dichotomy; we have to realize that in the final analysis whites *divided* the indigenous societies, they did not *unify* them, that this is a point-blank scientific fact. Walter Rodney, in his classic text *How Europe Underdeveloped Africa*, describes traditional African socio-political structures and provides a brilliant and extensive explanation of various dimensions of the dynamics of the continuing underdevelopment of Africa on the parts of Europeans and Euro-Americans. The UN announced in March, '08 that nearly two thirds of all Africans lack access to proper sanitation.

In my view there is nothing remotely benevolent about thinking *a priori* that indigenous societies were slave-driving warmongers before colonial influence. This projection expressed at least throughout the non-lumpen proletariat, industrialized western hemisphere is, of course, an expression of mass acute—Afrophobic—neuroses, which are contiguous with the European dissociation (typically expressed, at least among the bourgeois, as solipsisms) and accompanied by a broad spectrum of what the psychologist Alfred Adler would call "guiding fictions" (The phrase is fairly self-explanatory.) and by forms of narcissism—always compensatory, of course—that have conceit faces and self-hate faces.

As Adler explains in his classic *The Neurotic Constitution*, guiding fictions go hand-in-hand with neuroses. In the case of Afrophobia these guiding fictions are expressed by dispositions that range from the most overt white supremacism to the severe, covert Afrophobia of radical liberals who protest against Columbus Day. Realities, knowledge bases, even reason itself are atomized, and this atomization serves as a sort of platform from which epistemic violence and, of course, the worst forms of physical violence are issued. Those who are above the poverty level, having, as a collective (whether we look at white socialist workers or the black bourgeois, etc.), apparently never really put themselves into the struggle for justice for those who are below the poverty level, apparently tend to be comfortable with relativistic pluralism, which variously attempts and ostensibly attempts to integrate cultures, religions, etc. by atomizing them. Evidently they are rarely more than semi-conscious of any incentive to, as John Lennon might put it, "join the human race," despite the list of diverse, major crises they have caused in their own communities and so on. And again, when I speak of imperialism among non-lumpen proletariats *I am also speaking of a horrifically vast majority of radical liberal activists at large.*

In the U.S., for example, it is clear to see from the census data alone that holocausts are being committed against black American and many other cultures in the U.S. (The emphasis is on the innumerous *cultural* holocausts that are being committed against the last indigenous and quasi-indigenous cultures on earth.), yet the mass media continues to, at least largely, depict black Americans as though they are fully integrated into mainstream U.S. society, and whites, from the universities to the grocery stores, think that they are the only "race" that isn't an ethnic group. I am referring to the "ethnic studies departments" and the "ethnic foods isles". In terms of these two examples strictly it is infinitely more malignant and twisted. (Obviously ethnic studies classes are peripheral to "world history" classes, etc. (judging from factors like the way they are discussed by faculty and the proportion of students who enroll in them), yet one practically has to go to them to learn about the ancient Greeks' Kemetic teachers formally; and, of course, there are numerous case-studies of bizarre and irreverent political attacks of a peculiar sort against ethnic studies programs and professors and even just students and prospective students of color at universities throughout the U.S. since sometime around the early nineties. Public responses to these attacks have been telling.) There is scarcely any Africanist academic agitation of the quality we need in the U.S., *which is a case-in-point*, and the other neocolonialist countries—i.e., France, England, et al.—are, in terms of the underlying psychology, no better.

This Afrophobia runs its course in virtually every arena of non-lumpen proletariat society throughout at least the industrialized western hemisphere; it is invariably self-contradictory/neurotic and likewise takes the form of narcissism with a conceit face in white communities and unfortunately, increasingly since the early or mid-eighties narcissism with more of a self-hate face in lumpen proletariat communities. This self-hate induced by the schools, the mass/agenda-setting media, our therapists and psychiatrists, the prison industrial complex and, yes, non-lumpen proletariat society at large as a collective (with its glorification of the Greco-Roman tradition—including the whole supposedly evolutionary timeline from the turn of the common era to Mussolini apparently—and modern industrialization and its *a priori* stigmatization of indigenous societies) is, of course, a major cause of violent crime among people of color. The dominant power structure has to realize that, in the final analysis, whites are a far cry from being the be all, end all, and it has to admit publicly that its academia is basically upside-down on these various counts.

In order for the industrialized world as a collective to become individuated the people will have to turn academia right-side-up and/or create and maintain their own schools where the arts and sciences will be approached holistically and ethically, all sides will be heard and taken into account judicially and everything good will be integrated.

Expressions of the European dissociation among the black bourgeois have been mapped out pretty extensively in classic sources by scholars from Du Bois, Fanon and Huey Newton to Pamela Newkirk and Michael Eric Dyson. In fact, Du Bois wrote not long before he died that there was no hope for black America.

Anyone who was not a "Christian" was thought to be a pagan. Thus the myth that nonindustrial people were generally pagans began. This myth continues in popular academia to this day. It is embedded in the status quos of First World countries. It persists to such a degree that a small percent of any ethnic population seems to be aware of it.

Not only were indigenous people generally monotheists, like Christians, but, among tribes there were numerous systems of worshipping the Creator, and there were numerous names for the Creator, and there were various angels who were recognized, sometimes mutually among different tribes, sometimes exclusively within a single tribe or a single family. And this, contrary to popular hype, did not tend to cause wars.

Totemic systems, as Claude Levi-Strauss, the inventor of structural anthropology, has shown were usually geared to sustain harmonious socio-political relations among tribes. The totem of one tribe was intended to compliment that of another tribe. There was marrying between tribes. Slaves in indigenous cultures could also often marry within the tribe and participate in religious ceremonies, and they were not generally commodified the way they were with the European slave trade (Ohadike, 1994).

Most people in industrialized societies do not know words like *monopantheonism* or *matrifocal* for the same reason that they do not know words like *syllogism* or *holocaust*. A tragic array of ethnological stratification has resulted from this historical short-coming of European intelligence. Really, new agers continue to misinterpret ancient indigenous religions, to inadvertently portray them as being unconsciously nihilistic or solipsistic and non-monotheistic. Commonly the people who do claim to support or practice indigenous religions depict those religions entirely irresponsibly and inaccurately, which only helps Eurocentric scholars perpetuate their preconceptions.

In *From Afar to Zulu* rough accounts of the religions of twenty-four African tribes are given. Of the twenty-four eleven are presented as monotheists who exclusively worship a God as part of their own ancient religions. Ten are said to be mainly Christian, Jewish or Muslim monotheists. The former group is comprised of the Chokwe, Ewe, Kamba, Kikuyu, Kru, Maasai, Mbuti, Ndebele, Yoruba and Zulu. The latter group is comprised of the Baganda, Bemba, Falasha, Fang, Hausa, Kongo, Malinke, Tswana, Tutsi and Wolof.

This leaves three remaining tribes that do not fit into either category. They are generally described as ancestor and/or nature worshippers.

The depiction of indigenous people as primitive pagans, non-monotheists and empirically inferior has reared its ugly head in all areas of history and anthropology as well as all areas of psychology, from Freud to modern transpersonal theory. And not enough is being done about it academically. People of all ethnicities and cultural orientations are neither educating themselves nor talking about the less-known truths concerning these matters.

Geoffrey Parrinder's *African Mythology* (1973) says, "There is no doubt that nearly all, if not all, African peoples believe in a Supreme Being, the creator of

all things. A supreme god is named in the earliest dictionary of a Bantu language, compiled in 1650, and in Bosman's desription of West Africa published
in 1705. Belief in a Supreme Being is a thoroughly negro African conception,
current long before there were any established Christian or Moslem missions in
the interior regions of tropical or Southern Africa."

A.M. Lugira (1999) states, "In Western religion, religious systems are usually
classified as either monotheistic, that is, believing in one God, or polytheistic,
believing in many gods. In African religion, monotheism and polytheism exist
side by side. For a long time, scholars thought that African religion had always
been polytheistic only. They thought that the Supreme Being of African religion
was the result of contact with Christianity and Islam. We now know that this
is not the case. The African concept of one supreme God existed well before
Judaic, Christian or Islamic influence." He continues, "The African concept of
monotheism is one of a hierarchy, with the Supreme Being at its head. In this
system the Supreme Being rules over a vast number of divinities who are considered to be the associates of God. African understanding of the structure of
the heavenly kingdom might be compared to the Christian concept of God rul-
ing over the saints and angels. The divine hierarchy in African religion makes it
possible to classify them as both monotheistic and polytheistic at once. (monotheism with polytheism)."

Despite all of these sources, which conclusively show that most, if not all,
ancient African tribes were monotheists, the majority of documents available
today depict indigenous people as pantheonistic, nature and/or ancestor worshippers. Well, this is not the fault of indigenous people, it is the fault of historical and modern European anthropologists who have generally been unable to
tell the difference between pantheonism and monopantheonism or between
monotheism and monopantheonism, for that matter. They were unable to see
monotheism and pantheonism as compatible, despite the fact that Christianity,
for example, is itself monopantheonistic, whereas indigenous cultures have
generally never had any difficulty understanding monpantheonistic religion
or how it corresponds to cosmological principles. In addition, indigenous cultures commonly encrypted their religious and cosmological beliefs in myths
and folktales, which Europeans have historically failed to accurately decipher.
These are only a few examples of how European scholars have, due to their own
lack of intelligence (in some manner) historically underestimated the philosophical sophistication of indigenous cultures.[3]

---

3   I am not suggesting that all indigenous cultures had evolved psychologies. There
     have been a number of genuinely primitive indigenous cultures, some of which

These European predifferentiations are now deeply embedded, both consciously and unconsciously, in the status quos of First World countries. This is an extremely simple idea. At the same time it is one of the most difficult ideas to get across to common people, of any ethnicity. Monotheism means the belief in one Creator. Perfectly simple.

Pantheonism means the belief in several divine beings. Also perfectly simple. Pantheonism means any religion that reveres several divine beings; this means any divine beings. In other words, angels invariably comprise pantheons and pantheons are always comprised of angels. So, Christianity is as pantheonistic as most, nearly all, of the indigenous cultures which scholars generally refer to as "pagan," nature or ancestor worshipping or pantheonistic; and, likewise, most, nearly all, of these cultures are as monotheistic as Christians have ever been. Most people, of any ethnicity, do not know this. Why? They have been hardwired to not know it.

With the growing popularity of Eastern religions, Buddhism, Hinduism and Taoism, which are also monopantheonistic, scholars such as Wilber are willing to consider them to be monotheists. When we have tribes and drums and ecstatic ceremonial dances monotheists are called "pagans" by the same scholars.

It was not indigenous people who, as Wilber claims, were predifferentiative; it was Europeans who were predifferentiative. The means by which scholars have historically, through a double-standard, ascribed some monopantheonistic religions to pantheonism (or "paganism") and others to monotheism is the same means by which scholars have grossly misinterpreted the Bible. The same predifferentiation. It is also the same means by which metaphors have been misunderstood in all mythologies and in the Bible.

Most people who say they believe in ethnic equality don't know the first thing about any of this. The Christian pantheon, composed of the four archangels of the Hebrew Bible along with numerous Saints, is pictured (however consciously or otherwise) by most people as good. It is associated with gentle harp music and Christ who died on the cross. Eastern pantheons are associated with the wisdom that many people today have read in scriptures such as the Bhagavad Gita, works by Lao Tzu and Chuang Tzu and various Buddhist Sutras. So, Eastern pantheons are associated with that wisdom, with the remarkable technological advancements of the East and so on. All other pantheons are associated with tribes, scantly dressed people, drums, ecstatic dancing, the lack of written languages and so on, and with people who are generally darker than

---

are still existent, such as the Dobu who had an entirely cut-throat socio-political system.

Europeans or Easterners. All of this and much more makes it easier for scholars
to apply double standards to these issues.

The shaman is the individual who, within society, brings individual consciousness to those who do not have it. This is possible because the shaman's mindset
is first and foremost one of mercy and grace. When someone makes us angry,
jealous or afraid we often want to hurt that person in return. The shaman sees
that this is not necessary. It is not because the shaman expects something in
return. It is because this is his nature. He does not come from the physical.
He comes from the spiritual, which supersedes the physical. Because of this he
realizes preternaturally that it is necessary for everything in the physical world
to be in harmony. Since everything physical is intrinsically connected, to be
in harmony with anything is to be in harmony with yourself. This is both the
emotional and intellectual attitude of the shaman. He is a healer and a wise
man, able to tell those who are noble from those who are not. He knows the
compassion of the Supreme Being because he knows his own compassion.

The shaman is a holon too, like everything else that has a physical component. Being self-aware, he regards himself as a holon. This is to say he regards
himself as dependent on both the physical and the non-physical.

While the shaman is rational he also often practices kundalini yoga. Edward
Bruce Bynum writes in *The African Unconscious: Roots of Ancient Mysticism
and Modern Psychology* (1999), "It's most expansive expression is perhaps found
in the lineage of Kashmir Shaivism." Georg Feuerstein's *Encyclopedic Dictionary
of Yoga* is consistent with this statement. In the *Encyclopedic Dictionary of Yoga*
terms such as *Shaivism, hatha-yoga, kundalini, kundalini-yoga, kundalini-shakti,
magic, tantrism* and *moksha* are all contiguous with each other. Here is the definition for *Granthi*, "The Kathau Upanishad (VI. 15) again states that 'when
all the knots of the heart here [in the body] are cut, then a mortal becomes
immortal.' These knots are blockages in the axial current (sahasrara-cakra) and
prevent the 'serpent power' (kundalini-shakti) from ascending to the crown
center."

Numerous supporting definitions are given throughout the book. The idea
is to raise kundalini energy—which is, in its mundane form, simply sexual
energy—from the base chakra, Shakti, to the crown chakra, Siva. According to
the *Encyclopedic Dictionary of Yoga* and its sources this is the way to liberation.[4]
In Hinduism it is believed that this practice can entail the ability to transcend

---

4   Feuerstein not only conducted a, by European standards, incomparable amount of
     research for the book, he also spoke with some of the Mahatmas.

the laws of physics. Levitation and the ability to visit non-corporeal planes of being are often referred to.

This practice is described in many ways and accounts of the experiences associated with it are generally inconsistent with each other. Many texts—most notably from Kashmir, where Kashmir Shaivism originated—were destroyed or lost, and many others have not been translated or have only recently been translated. The Siva Sutras, translated into English for the first time in the nineties by Jadaeva Singh, especially the Paratrisika Vavarana, are identical to the pyramid texts originally translated by R.O. Faulkner. Faulkner is well known for his translation of *The Egyptian Book of the Dead*.

Bynum refers to Faulkner's The *Ancient Egyptian Pyramid Texts* in *The African Unconscious*. Nelson gives a great account of sixth chakra consciousness in *Healing the Split*, complete with various information such as how it relates to second chakra regressions.

Wilber associates his sixth—"subtle," "soul"—level with mantras and his seventh—"causal," "spirit"—level with self-reflection. None of these forms of meditation have anything to do with anything higher than the fifth chakra. In Kashmir Shaivism there is a degree of discipline necessary that would make practitioners of other forms of meditation either cringe or simply not believe it is possible. Kashmir Shaivism is the form of meditation which coincides with the transcendence of physical desires. This is why Nelson explains that before one can proceed with the attainment of the sixth chakra they must be able to sustain their ego.

Just as the rational level, chakras three through five, is the necessary bridge between the prerational and transrational levels, so the rational level (eros) must be sufficiently maintained before it can be transcended. Of course it is always necessary to have sexual ethics. Sexual ethics are perhaps explained best in Da Free John's section *Transcending the Sexual Limits of East and West* from his book *Scientific Proof of the Existence of God Will Soon be Announced from the Whitehouse* (1985). The type of polygamy that Da Free John describes, however, is exemplified in cultures like that of the Maasai, not in any known historical or modern European culture.

The libido must be transcended systematically. Ultimately any attempt to completely transcend it without a regimen of authentic kundalini yoga will result in repression. People do not understand Kashmir Shaivism because it is the way to transcend physical desires.

Strangely, Wilber actually becomes personic at the sixth chakra (or what he calls the seventh level). It is somewhat complicated how this occurs. Basically

Wilber seems to renounce "gross-body" responsibilities at what he calls the seventh level and contiguously confuses various basic attributes of the sixth chakra with those of his supposed higher seventh level.

Other forms of meditation aim at nothing more than experiences of the infinite interconnectedness between ones ego and everything else, holonic aperspectival consciousness (usually unconsciously). Emptiness of form is a phenomenological idea. When we experience it it is called *sunyata*. Wilber says that this is the eighth level. Really it is only a form of satori. The belief that sunyata is the ultimate state of enlightenment can be mostly ascribed to Subhuti who was one of the ten great disciples of the Buddha. In kundalini yoga the feeling is that we are beginning to supersede our egos and everything else.

At the fifth chakra we have metaphysics, which—although infinite in a sense—are based on a physical ontology. Thus there is still latent eros, and all of the states of oneness that are available there are, on the unconscious level, holonic. At the sixth chakra we begin to transcend physical desires. Thus we begin to transcend holonic states of consciousness. Furthermore fifth chakra expressions, like those of all egoic chakras and of the second, are generally extensions of the libido. Jung realized that his archetypes were extensions of the libido. Most great scholars throughout history have likewise been aware of the libidinous aspects of their respective systems of logic. None of the visions that are attainable through sixth chakra consciousness involve the libido or the ego. This is why Nelson makes the insightful discernment between Jungian archetypes and sixth chakra archetypes.

In short, I believe that kundalini yoga is the way to liberation. It is esoterically known as the Short Path and the Nine Stages of Calming the Mind. With the ascension to each higher chakra there is a radical increase in consciousness. The first chakra is survival instincts and our connection to the earth. The second chakra is procreation. The third chakra is emotional vitality and empirical logic. The fourth is the first altruistic chakra and the beginning of metaphysical reasoning. This is to say, it is also empirical, but at the higher stages there is incomplete metaphysical thought. At the pinnacle of the fourth chakra are figures such as Socrates and Carl Jung. The fifth chakra is where a fundamental understanding of metaphysical reasoning begins, psychological and potentially mathematical. This is mandalic consciousness. Hermeneutics, dream symbols, math, synchronistic events, any symbols. This eventually happens at the fifth chakra. To whatever extent this capacity is exercised depends on many factors. As Salvador Dali said, "Inventiveness is the key to survival." This is true at the fifth chakra. Meditation is also important, zazen and so on. At the beginning of the sixth chakra there is also mandalic consciousness. But this is eventually out-moded. If it were not the growth of awareness contiguous with the sixth com-pared to the fifth would not be in proportion to that of each previous chakra in relation to those immediately below them.

At each chakra the consciousness of the next is usually thought to be impos-sible. Those at the second chakra cannot typically imagine empirical reasoning. Those at the third chakra are generally unable to appreciate altruism. Those at the fourth chakra are rarely receptive to the idea of ontological awareness that marks the transition into fifth chakra consciousness. (I recommend Laing's *The Politics of Experience* for documentation of the phenomena associated with this transition.)

Since mere psychic perception is still subjective and thus symbolic, it is not much of a step up from fifth chakra consciousness. At the sixth chakra one also begins to simply intuit accurately how things are. This transcends syllogistic thinking, but it still is not a sufficient evolutionary step. It is not as distinct as the transitions from chakras one to two, two to three, three to four or four to five. All of the definitive texts from Egypt and India, as well as contemporary sources, say that sexual restraint is necessary to the cultivation of sixth chakra consciousness. The only step that would make sense, considering the differ-ences between each chakra up to the fifth, would be, not only clairvoyance but the beginning of the transcendence of the ego itself. Logic (the ego) has already been essentially carried to its far limits at the fifth chakra. It is with the fifth chakra that Einstein assisted two other men in the release of atomic energy. Space travel isn't even fifth chakra, It's fourth, at the highest. Fifth chakra logic is basically as far as the ego can go. It is at the fifth chakra that we eventually understand the divine order of the universe. We map out the most esoteric laws of cause and effect. Anything that the ego can accomplish can be accomplished at the fifth chakra. Therefore the sixth chakra must, at some point, entail the transcendence of the ego.

Although scholars such as Bynum and Nelson are in thorough agreement with this, and Feuerstein's *Encyclopedic Dictionary of Yoga* and its sources say the same thing, there are some profound dilemmas in current theories of spiritual evolution. Perhaps the two books that present this dilemma most are Wilber's *Up From Eden* and Feuerstein's *Structures of Consciousness: The Genius of Jean Gebser*. In both of these books the rise of monotheism supposedly coincided with the Bronze Age, 2,500 B.C. in Europe and the Near-East. Supposedly humans until then did not have "accumulative" consciousness or superegos. This was also, they say, when patriarchy began. In *Up From Eden*, which was published first, Wilber has a circular diagram of vertical evolution that consists of eight stages, which go as follows: 1) uruboric, 2) typhonic, 3) mythic-membership (matriarchal, pantheonistic), 4) the solar ego (patriarchal, monotheistic), 6) subtle (The Great Goddess), 7) causal (The Father), 8) God-Head (Sunyata). The third level, which is matriarchal, corresponds to the sixth level, which is also feminine. The fourth level, which is patriarchal, corresponds to the seventh level, which is also masculine.

Typhons were "subhuman." Mythic-membership individuals, since they supposedly represented the beginning of praxis, "verbal membership," were human but were matriarchal, including the most unlikely candidates of the era like dynastic Egypt, and did not have the same self-reflective reasoning as people began to have "in Europe and the Near East" at about the beginning of the Bronze Age. In nineteen-hundred B.C. in Persia for example a fairly refined form of monotheism was developed. This supposedly coincided with Christianity, technology, the written word, i.e. Herodotus and Homer. According to Wilber the solar-ego represents a stronger sense of self-identity, what the scholar of Buddhism Robert Thurman might call "ego-definition". Everything prior to about 2,000 B.C. was premonotheistic in Wilber's view, and this premonotheism was contiguous with matriarchy. This was also why "pre-industrial" societies did not have written languages. Actually, as Asante writes, "Writing has been prominent in Africa among priests and royalty. The adinkra ideograms of the Asante, the nsibidi of the Ejagham, and the sacred symbols of the Benin Obas are but a few examples of African writing. None of the early African writing systems owe anything to Western systems."

In Wilber's theory typhonic subhumans and mythic-membership individuals were all essentially matriarchal, whether they were ruled by sovereign kings or worshipped prominently male divinities, whether misogyny dominated their societies or the main archetypal imagery expressed traditionally was of or related to light, the sun, the sky (all symbols which, in any other context, Wilber calls the "solar logos," which connotes the solar-ego level). Tribes like the Maasai and the Kikuyu, for example, call the Supreme *Ngai*, which means sky. Throughout West Africa, in places like Yorubaland royal stools are some of the most revered spiritual objects, and they are said to be symbolic of stools which originally came from the sky. Sun and light symbolism pervades African mythology, folktales, poetry and oral tradition in general. A high ratio of hero myths has also existed in Africa since before colonization.

One way that Wilber arrives at this model is by ascribing kundalini yoga to only the typhonic and membership stages, so that the typhon was able reach—at the highest—the fifth level, and the people during the mythic-membership period were able to reach no higher than the sixth level. According to Wilber, there were "shamans" as far back as the typhonic (paleolithic) age, 200,000 to 12,000 B.C.—and they practiced rudimentary kundalini yoga and could arrive at trance states. This was at most in the realm of psychic abilities. During the mythic-membership period, 12,000 to 2500 B.C. (Feuerstein has 30,000 to 2500 B.C.) people also practiced kundalini yoga (hence the depiction of the sixth chakra in dynastic Egypt) and they were able to reach nothing beyond the beginning of the sixth level.

He equates kundalini yoga with nirmanakaya, the first of the three kayas. Kaya means "body." In Vajrayana Buddhism there are three kayas: nirmana-kaya, samboghogakaya and dharmakaya. Kundalini yoga did not originate in any Buddhist tradition. I have spoken with numerous scholars of Buddhism and tried to find literature about this. None of the scholars, some of whom had been studying nirmanakaya for over twenty years, had heard of any relation between kundalini and any of the kayas. It was easier to find texts about the yoga of intermediate state and rebirth. The closest thing to any relation between yoga and nirmanakaya Buddhism was in texts such as *The Six Yogas of Naropa* by Garma Chang. Such texts have practically nothing in common with ancient Egyptian or Hindu sources. Vajrayana Buddhism is Tibetan, and Tibet was conquered by Mongolians in the sixteenth century. As a result, Tibetan traditions, having already gone through significant changes, became far more diluted. Later that century shamanism would no longer be an accepted part of the religion. For instance, I like the 14th Dalai Lama, but he has rightly criticized many former Dalai Lamas and other prominent figures of the Vajrayana lineage. There is much that is good in modern Tibetan Buddhism, but it is patriarchal, and there has been a significant amount of corruption over the centuries. Besides, Wilber doesn't even particularly subscribe to astrology, and Patriarchs in Tibetan Buddhism are generally decided with astrology and similar means of supposed divination. *The Shambhala Dictionary of Buddhism and Zen* does not have the word kundalini in it. Nor do any Buddhist dictionaries that I know of. Likewise there is nothing about any kind of yoga under nirmanakaya in any of these dictionaries. *The Shambhala Dictionary of Buddhism and Zen* has, for instance, patriarchy, but not matriarchy. Actually, the closest thing to Kashmir Shaivism in any Buddhist tradition is the yoga of intermediate state and rebirth.

For some reason Wilber and Feuerstein both contradicted Feuerstein's own book. There are many other factors that they have missed as well in order to arrive at ethnologically distorted views of human evolution. I will give an overview of these in the following sections.

Wilber subscribes to Swami Muktananda's views expressed in *The Play of Consciousness*, and to Sri Aurobindo's expressed in *The Synthesis of Yoga*. Here we arrive at somewhat complicated issues. Kundalini yoga is only supposed to go up to the beginning of the sixth level (soul) at the highest. Yet Wilber says that Kashmir Shaivism is seventh level (spirit). But Kashmir Shaivism is what the Egyptians practiced. The Play of Consciousness does not describe anything like nirmanakaya, nor like most texts, is it particularly consistent with other accounts of kundalini yoga. The *Encyclopedic Dictionary of Yoga* clearly separates Aurobindo's yoga from Kashmir Shaivism. If Kashmir Shaivism corresponds to spirit and nirmanakaya does not, how is nirmanakaya kundalini yoga? Wilber knows about the Siva Sutras too. Somehow these scholars have managed to brush all of this aside and completely contradict themselves. This is one way that they have arrived at their patriarchal, Eurocentric conclusions.

Shamanism, as Wilber states, does not exist prior to sixth chakra consciousness. Fifth chakra modes can also be utilized, but they are utilized first from a sixth chakra reference point. The shaman was not only, as Wilber says, "the most highly evolved individual of typhonic times." The shaman is the most highly evolved human of any era.

Jaynes concedes that invariably "ancient poetry is much closer to song." He also writes of poetry, "What unseen light leads us to such dark practice?" He states that speech is a function of the left hemisphere and music is a function of the right hemisphere. His huge, unmistakable blunder (in this of many instances) is that he associates poetry, which obviously exemplifies balance between the two hemispheres, with the bicameral mind. He starkly associates imbalance between the two hemispheres with normal, healthy consciousness. This disproves his theory. Similarly he gives numerous examples of solarization in "bicameral" civilizations, which makes the fact that Wilber based his mythic-membership theory on Jaynes' views of mythology entirely ridiculous. What Jaynes defines as schizophrenia is, in turn, primarily the balance between the two hemispheres. This was the message of Laing and Levi-Strauss. Jaynes work is full of what Akbar would call "grafted consciousness."

He states that prayer did not exist in strictly bicameral times, that it was the result of consciousness. Prayers, he claims, were not common until the first millennium B.C. Then he blatantly contradicts his theory by saying, "Persons who have attended church regularly since childhood are more susceptible to hypnosis."

In hypnosis there is an obvious interface between that part of the individual's unconscious that is most susceptible to commands and that part of the individual that performs what is necessary given their "physical" surroundings.

The most functional terms for the former and latter locations of the individual are ethereal and realm of earth, air, fire and water respectively. This manner of categorizing the locations of the psyche-soma was known of by most ancient civilizations and is documented in, for example, esoteric Hindu metaphysics.

There is much about hypnosis that we do not understand. We do not understand, for example, how an individual can overcome severe pain and will, at once, walk around a physical chair unconsciously if told that the chair is not there. What we do know is that in hypnosis people absolutely have a subjective (though basically physiologically unconscious) perception of linear (sequential) time.

We also know that the part of the unconscious that is most susceptible to commands in hypnosis is the same part that is susceptible to any other psychosomatic influences. People are programmable, but the "programming" (hypnosis and other psychosomatic influences) does not take place consciously. It does not even take place in a non-physiologically conscious manner.

One of the functions of dreams is to report states and events that the individual would not be potentially conscious of per se. Anything that the individual is thinking or learning in a cognitive, unconscious manner can (theoretically) be reported to the physiologically conscious mind through dream symbolism. By dream symbolism I mean both dreams and surrealism.

Dream symbolism is the means by which we potentially overcome (unconscious) programming. Ancient cultures understood this. The practice of hypnotism, historically, is epitomically congruent with the European and Indo-European dissociation of the soma. Ancient cultures, especially African, where obedient to the messages of their physiologically unconscious minds. They had relatively profound senses of the natural oneness of psyche and soma. This is why Osiris descended from the sky to earth and the Assyrian angels ascended from earth to the sky. If Africans had been as prone to hypnotism as white people are they wouldn't have survived slavery.

In actual hypnotism, where one is physiologically unconscious, one is not aware of their physical surroundings. This is one of the clearest reasons for the implausibility of the theory of the bicameral mind.

We should also note that Jaynes uses phrases like "it is possible" and "it may be" continually throughout his book. He uses these phrases to an eerie extent. And in his words hypnotism is partly a matter of presenting "an *as-if* with a suppression of an *it-isn't*." He employs this and numerous other equally insidious tactics throughout his book. All of this in order to convince the reader that poetry and music are specifically associated with the bicameral mind, war is specifically associated with the appearance of consciousness, the ancient Olmec pyramids are "clumsy," the rules of logic are "not the way the mind works" and so forth.

He writes, "The picture of a scientist sitting down with his problems and using conscious induction and deduction is as mythical as a unicorn." If this were true the greatest scientific theories would have been produced under hypnosis and we would do better without consciousness. Nearly everything Jaynes writes about science definitely applies to his work, but not to actual, objective science.

In short, abundant and eclectic evidence suggests that monotheism, the concept of laws of nature, et al. all originated in ancient Africa. But in ancient African societies, *as in other ancient monopantheonistic societies*, religion *integrated and transcended* philosophy, psychology, etc. *The Supreme Being—Spirit—and divinities—spirits—were viewed both religiously and syllogistically.*

Priests in most traditional African societies prior to colonial influence were probably at the fifth chakra. A good number of them were probably at the sixth, and some of them may have been at the seventh.

Chakras three through five however are the only egoic chakras. We can speak rationally about chakras one and two (the prerational chakras), because we have integrated and transcended them at the third chakra and "higher". But we cannot prove anything transrational—sixth and seventh chakra consciousness. So, I will not make any assertions regarding the sixth or seventh chakra; that would be dogma.

Judging from the similarities between religions from throughout traditional Africa (Bantu, Akan, Yoruba, Igbo, Shona, et al.), Taoism, Buddhism, Hinduism (Taoism and Buddhism have become increasingly elevationistic (ptf-2) since fairly early A.D., though the 14th Dalai Lama writes prodigiously about traditional Buddhist thought in *A Policy of Kindness* (Piburn (Ed.), 1993), and so on. But traditional Hindu thought has been preserved extensively and with notable virtuosity even in recent times by Indian scholars like Radhakrishnan and Raman. (Unfortunately, despite this, Vaisnavas and Hare Krsnas, etc. in countries like the U.S. evidently generally do not know or care the least bit who the Dravidians or the dalits are. This is also despite the fact that *Krsna* translates from Sanskrit literally as *black, et al.*)), Judaism and Native American, Oceanic and other indigenous religions, etc., it has for at least the past several millennia—and probably since cir. 50,000 B.C. or even much earlier—been natural for *homo sapiens sapiens* to subscribe to *monopantheonistic* religions in which syllogistic reasoning, both empirical and metaphysical, is integrated and transcended.

CHAPTER THREE

Ecology

It is necessary to place the major waves of hegemonious documentations in the context of their origins and their histories. This requires a considerable ability to hone in on more authentic counter information and to explain what makes this information valid. Among the libraries of stratification, which consist largely as social mechanisms, as the products of numerous individuals, rather than lending themselves to the allocations of particular individuals in every case, there have been throughout the history of the written word, and are increasingly, as products of modern awareness, documents that provided grounded and detailed accounts of the less-known truth. Two subjects that I feel are delicately interwoven with the subject of ecology are racism and sexism as they have existed and do exist in popular academia. For this reason I will dissect these issues in adequate detail in this chapter.

Audre Lorde writes:

> "Ignoring differences between women and the implications of those differences presents the most serious threat to the mobilization of women's joint power.... An example of this is the signal absence of the experiences of women of Color as a resource for women's studies courses.... All too often the excuse given is that the literatures of women of Color can only be taught by Colored women, or that they are difficult to understand, or that classes cannot 'get into' them because they come out of experiences that are 'too different.' ... And I believe this holds true for other women of Color who are not Black."

This sentiment is echoed by virtually all prominent black authors of feminism—Angela Davis, June Jordan, bell hooks, Patricia Hill Collins, Oyeronke Oyewumi, Mojubaolu Olufunke Okome, et al.

Nepalese indigenous women's rights leader Stella Tamang seems to speak for at least the vast majority of all indigenous women's rights leaders globally when she states, "*The international women's movement does not represent indigenous women*." (my italics.)

Scholars like Collins have pointed out the racism, classism, etc. of popular white feminists like Nancy Chodorow and Carol Gilligan. *Mainstream and popular authors of feminism also generally express the European solipsism acutely, not to mention a lot of standard—malignant—neocolonialist doublespeak, etc.*

We are to believe that the ancestors of the same men responsible for two World Wars at one time, typically designated to the eras before the Bronze Age (2500 B.C.), worshipped women. The usual explanations for this are that before the Bronze Age men did not understand procreation, thus women were considered magical because of their ability to give birth, there were 55 female figurines versus 5 male figurines found at prehistoric sites in Europe (The Trust for African Rock Art (TARA) was not founded until 1996.), etc. Wilber and other prominent scholars today have perpetuated this misconception.

Wilber has probably presented the most elaborate promulgation of the myth of matriarchal prehistory. And, despite his explicit denial of his Eurocentrism and patriarchy, the paradigm he presents is inarguably thoroughly Eurocentric and patriarchal. In his Four Quadrants paradigm (which is in the front of a number of his books), in the lower right quadrant, he places indigenous societies—ostensibly *ancient* indigenous societies exclusively, however exactly this dichotomy is supposed to function—two and three distinct hierarchal levels below industrial societies and three and four distinct hierarchal levels below informational societies. (Whatever can be said about his "lines of development" (which are a shambles, incidentally), these hierarchical levels are basically distinct.) He went to great lengths to support this view, claiming that when transitions were made from horticultural to agrarian modes of subsistence patriarchy became necessary because it is a "medical fact" that when women draw heavy plows it greatly increases the risk of miscarriages, and so on. Obviously, women do not have to draw heavy plows to contribute as much or much more than men to the subsistence sphere in an agrarian society (Rosaldo and Lamphere (Eds.), 1974), *et al.* (The hegemony of scholars like Wilber and Habermas does not hold up any better empirically than it does metaphysically.)

Cynthia Eller, in her book *The Myth of Matriarchal Prehistory: Why an Invented Past Won't Give Women a Future* (2000), has conclusively debunked the myth of matriarchal prehistory in all of its expressions. She traced its origins from ancient Greece, where it was propagated by patriarchs, to its revival by Johann

Jacob Bachofen in 1861, through its treatment by scholars since (mostly men who tried to use it to support the idea of male superiority), up to its feminist origins in Merlin Stone's *The Paradise Papers* (1976), later titled *When God was a Woman*, and Marija Gimbuta's *The Gods and Goddesses of Old Europe* (1974), later titled *The Goddesses and Gods of Old Europe*. She traced the largest supposed sites, from Catalhoyuk to Minoan Crete to Malta, India, England and Ireland, and exhaustively maintains how the misconception began, whether or not particular artifacts were indicative of goddess worship at all (which, in many popular cases, they were not), what any goddess worship that did exist prehistorically would connote about the status of women in those societies according to anthropological and sociological research, linguistic evidence of a patriarchal proto-Indo-European language, and so on. Perfectly extensive and brilliant. She has accomplished a work which should have been taken on by a large number of writers.

The following passage from Monica Sjoo and Barbara Mor's *The Great Cosmic Mother* (1987) is evidently reflective of the general views of the myth of matriarchal prehistory expressed, "The Moon Goddess was worshipped in orgiastic rites, being the divinity of matriarchal women free to take as many lovers as they chose. Women could surrender themselves to the Goddess by making love to a stranger in her temple. This has been called by male historians 'sacred prostitution,' but the word is totally misleading. This was not any kind of service to men, nor did women have to do this to live …"

The authors say that this was a way to "*enlarge* the woman's ego-consciousness into an experience of cosmic sexual power and flow." (My italics.)

The main proponents of this global subculture's (Eller makes it very clear that it is a global subculture.) works are all full of pre/trans fallacies. They inarguably go way, way out of their ways to put ancient Egypt in the shadow of Sumer. They say that they're not glorifying patriarchy in reverse, but they obviously are, *et al.*

Stone calls these imagined prehistoric societies "matriarchal" societies, Gimbutas calls them "matristic". *For all means and purposes these "matriarchal" and "matristic" societies bare no resemblance to any historical or contemporary matrifocal or matrilineal society that I know of.*

As Eller points out, geographically the myth of matriarchal prehistory is for the most part restricted to Europe and the Near East. *These are the two most genealogically European geographies, in terms of ancient history, and they are the two that have the least to do with historical or existent matrifocal or matrilineal societies.*

Polyandry seems to have been extremely rare in traditional African societies, etc.

In my view, mainstream and popular feminism is more or less the watermark. When European feminists and feminists of European extraction, collectively, are covertly violently oppressive toward their indigenous sisters and sisters of color it shows just how bereft of character or honest intentions the non-lumpen proletariat masses in the First World are collectively.

Eller is an example of a new breed of academic writers. I speculate that there is a pattern occurring. While doing research for this book most of the useful information I was able to find was in books that were copyrighted since 1999. These books are based often and necessarily on more incisive and thorough investigations into matters which have often been historically kept from the public. What defines these new writers are entirely new modes of intelligence and courage. They are nothing less than warriors, for they are a minority in an age where self-education is of paramount importance.

Most accounts, to this day, insist that Europeans and Indo-Europeans were the leaders of civilization. The truth is that cultures throughout the world were, by and large, equal in their developments, religiously, sociologically, linguistically, taxonomically, architecturally, and in terms of art, agriculture, clothes and craftsmanship. The only ways that Europe and the Near East surpassed most other regions were militaristically and by way of the written word. After scholars from Du Bois to Cesaire, from West to Bynum, it is a mystery how Wilber and others can continue to propagate Eurocentric and patriarchal myths. The best source I know of for information about historical African accomplishments, other than Egyptian, is the eighth chapter, titled *African Culture*, of Du Bois' *The Negro* (1915). In this chapter, which is thirty-nine pages in length, depending on the copy, he extols elaborate documentation from numerous European and other anthropological sources, mostly from the nineteenth century, but some from as early as twelfth century India. He explains laconically and judicially that African culture at large, since its earliest history has been far more advanced than many would have us think. On many counts their craftsmanship and modes of socio-politics were superior to those of Europe. He gives convincing evidence of the idea that black Africans were the original craftsmen and exporters of iron.

Racism has taken on the subtlest and most elusive forms, it has also taken on the most overt and barbaric forms. Numerous philosophers, from Voltaire to Hume to Hegel to Kant were racists. At the same time Frank Snowden says that the ratio of biased to unbiased ethnological accounts by prominent scholars in classical literature was more or less equal. Herodotus said that Ethiopians were the most handsome people on earth. In *The History* (2.104) he describes the Egyptians as "dark-skinned and woolly-haired." He describes Ethiopian

Egyptian kings, etc. He and numerous other ancient historians—i.e., Homer, Pythagoras, Isocrates, Plutarch, Plato, Aristotle, etc.—testified that the Greeks learned a huge amount of what they knew about mathematics, metaphysics, etc. from the ancient Egyptians.

Homer wrote:

> "Of visage solemn, sad, but sable hue,
> short, wooly curls, o'erfleeced his bending head, …
> Eurybiates, in whose large soul alone,
> Ulysses viewed an image of his own."

Here is a passage by Homer about the ancient Nubian kingdom:

> "They are the remotest of nations,
> the most just of men,
> the favorite of the gods.
> The lofty inhabitants of Olympus
> journey to them to take part
> in their feasts."

Until the twentieth century the consensus among scholars was that Egypt was not even part of Africa. Some scholars still consider Egypt to be part of the Near East. Wilber tries to dismiss dynastic Egypt as matriarchal by overemphasizing the role of Isis and so on, even though most Egyptian deities were depicted as males. Dynastic Egypt was not matriarchal. For the most part it was not patriarchal either. This was not due to pre-differentiation either. Egyptian civilization, throughout most of the dynastic period, was one of the most advanced societies ever, and its roots were in black Africa.

Indo-Europeans are Europeans with a slight African genetic influence. They often have Africoid hair, full noses and lips and dark, olive complexions. With ancient Egyptians there is the reverse. They were Africans with slight European genetic influences. They did not usually have facial hair. The goatee-looking things were horse hair. While there were many depictions of light-skinned people with relatively slim features, Egyptians were mostly shown having broad bone structures, wide skulls from their foreheads to their brows, to their cheekbones and mastoids. Their noses and lips were typically African. They were often depicted with literally black skin. The royalty especially were usually, clearly African. Aside from this, Egyptian hieroglyphs had nothing in common with any hieroglyphs from the Near East. Rather, there are symbols on pottery and such from other areas of ancient North Africa that look as though they might have been what Egyptian hieroglyphs were derived from. Many scholars, including many (probably most) members of the NABP, believe that Nubia was the mother of Egypt. There are obvious similarities between the ancient Nubian Kingdom and dynastic Egypt. And the ancient Nubian population was, unlike that of dynastic Egypt, more or less exclusively black Also *Egyptian* does come from the Greek *Aiguptos*, which means black.

The most incisive discussion of the gene-pool of ancient Egypt that I know of is Finch's introduction to *African Background to Medical Science*, which is cited along with numerous other similarly penetrating sources in *The African Unconscious*.

Joseph Greenberg, a pioneering linguist, has broken down all languages into seventeen groups. Four of these are African. Ancient Egyptian, according to Greenberg, is in the Afro-Asiatic group, which spanned from the Near East across most of the upper half of Africa—as well as through Kenya, Somalia, Ethiopia and Eritrea—to the west coast. Remember, this is where numerous texts say that ancient trade routes existed. Early rock art in Algeria, for example, has been noted by paleontologists as resembling popular designs from dynastic Egypt. Also, most people in north-east Africa, like the ancient Egyptians, do not have facial hair. The Afro-Asiatic group comprises approximately 240 languages. Its number of speakers, among African language groups, is equaled only by the Niger-Kordofanian group, each comprising roughly 180 million speakers. The Afro-Asiatic group includes Hebrew and Aramaic, which means that the entire Old Testament was written in branches of an essentially North African language group.

We know that Egyptians exchanged material goods and information with other African societies throughout northern Africa, all the way to the west coast (Davidson, 1968, 1974, et al.) and with societies to the east, most notably the Dravidian Harappan/Indus civilization of pre-Aryan India. The Harappan civilization was founded around 2500 B.C. The Harappans populated vast cities that looked much like modern cities, with wide roads, multi-storied buildings, pyramid structures, irrigation and sewage systems and so on. They had a written script comprised of somewhere between 400 and 450 symbols that did not owe anything to any other known script; they had schools, various toys, including dice that looked like modern dice, et al. Notably, there are many depictions of unicorns among Harappan artifacts (Bynum, 1999; Ratnagar, 2006; Basham, 1963; Oppert, 1978, *et al.*).

Most of the trade between Egypt and the Harappan civilization was conducted by sea (Bynum, 1999; Ratnagar, 2006, *et al.*). The semi-nomadic Aryans colonized the Harappans cir. 1500 B.C. and plagiarized various religious ideas and iconography and at least some integral metaphysical ideas in the Vedas (Oppert, 1978; Radhakrishnan, 1966; Deppert (Ed.), 1983). They also introduced the caste system.

For much more extensive information on the Dravidian pre-Aryan Indians and their capital and trade see *The African Unconscious* and Shereen Ratnagar's *Trading Encounters*. There is an abundance of valuable and very accessible sources on the Harappan civilization. Even today dictionaries say that the Dravidians of ancient India were "Australoid". It is obvious from contemporary research on Y chromosomes and for various other reasons that the population of India before the Aryans invaded was predominantly black and Africoid (Bayly (Ed.), 1990, et al.).

There are some bases that are important to the paradigm presented in this book that are covered particularly well in *The African Unconscious*, throughout which there are exquisite citations of sources on subjects like early agrarian societies in the Nile River valley, dispersions of genes, phenotypes, etc. globally, black Africoid people in early dynastic China and throughout Asia in general throughout history and so on.

This book is intended to complement existing scholarship, and dominant academics should already be caught up well enough on classic sources by scholars like Du Bois, Finch, Obenga, Rodney, Jahn, Davidson, Senghor, Horton, Ohadike, Gyekye, Umeh, Stokely Carmichael, Newton, Davis, Herskovits, Levi-Strauss, Jung, et al. For that matter, they should, of course, have some iota as to what the ancient Greeks—the supposed fountainheads of their own Greco-Roman tradition—said about the Egyptians and Nubians and other black Africans. Industrialized societies will not be civilized until it is common knowledge at our colleges that Egyptians who were at least predominantly black invented geometry and whatnot. Representatives of the dominant power structure continue to act and speak as though these subjects are still hotly debated when they were buried ages ago, *conclusively*, scientifically, syllogistically. A certain amount of collective rationale is necessary to the creation or maintenance of any civilization. Where is the semblance of competence in the corporate state, the police state, the prison industrial complex, in clinical psychology or psychiatry, in our schools, among non-lumpen proletariat liberal activists, in these various spheres of Afrophobic society?

For example, only about one million people signed the online petition to impeach Bush W. by 2008; there are more than 381 million people in the U.S., and *tens of millions* of people typically call in on the TV show *American Idol* in a single night. No imperialist is camouflaged per se given this type of phenomena.

It has always been acute neuroses and not simple mean spiritedness that has driven imperialism and fascism. Thinkers from Fanon to Newton have been acutely conscious of and explicit about this fact. We can see imperialism as neuroses if we look at, say, the letters of white Union soldiers during the U.S. Civil War or accounts of radical white liberal activists during the sixties. There are whites doing some sincere stuff in relation to the Bioneers and whatnot, but those above the poverty level, as a collective, are far too acutely neurotic to unite, organize and mobilize that effectively for the major causes they say they stand for. At the same time, it is important to note that black Americans, since the early or mid-eighties, have been capitulating on an unprecedented, overwhelming and rapidly growing scale. These mass neuroses must be answered with mass psychotherapy (Pharmaceuticals evidently are not working that well.), which brings us back to refined Africanist academic agitation, which there is scarcely any of in countries like the U.S.

I am trying to communicate the fact that even the typical non-lumpen proletariat liberal activist irreverently issues mountains of malignant epistemic violence toward actual progressives. So, there is a certain emphasis on the relation between imperialism as neuroses, what Adler calls guiding fictions and epistemic violence.

By assimilating one can often gain access to new worlds of economic, legal and social power. The struggle has always been a spiritual and metaphysical struggle. Colonialist and neocolonialist societies have always been, first and foremost, anti-metaphysical. This is why it is necessary to the survival of the *homo sapiens sapiens* species as we know it that cultures that integrate the soma, feeling, the unconscious, intergenerational consciousness, hemispheric balance, a sense of ones own positive agency, reverence for the *other* in general, be preserved and revered.

It should be thoroughly obvious to non-lumpen proletariats at large that we are in an Orwellian situation, that soylent green is people; so, they must take it upon themselves to make sure that honest texts—psychology, history, sociology, anthropology, archeology, et al.—are distributed everywhere, *especially to lumpen proletariat areas*, since it is no secret on the black side of academia that those are the areas where people will listen infinitely more often. It could not be more obvious that all of the global crises that the non-lumpen proletariat masses claim to be outraged about are rooted in the Eurocentrism in our schools. We need discussions and debates between representatives of dominant academia and leading progressive black and indigenous scholars—in the public eye.

Bynum has done an enormous amount to bring various data about Africa together. Using several authoritative references in *The African Unconscious* he shows that there were trade routes throughout ancient Africa. Some of them were along rivers that traveled west from the Nile. This may have been before dynastic Egypt. Here is an excerpt:

> "It should be remembered that the Sphinx was ancient even in Egyptian-Nubian times, no one knowing who built it or when! From the water erosion markings at its base, the limestone figure was carved when the Sahara was lush with rivers, lakes and rainfall, at least 10,000 to 8000 B.C.E., long before the first known dynasties. It was dug from the sand and partially repaired by rulers who were mystified by its appearance even back then. Diop has intimated an ancient civilization; so has Schwaller de Lubicz (1961). Serpent in the Sky (West, 1970) boldly suggests the existence of a high civilization prior to Kemet as we know it. Since there were no Greeks or Romans of this time and Abraham of the Jews and Muslims lived millennia later, the only possible people this could have emerged from were the indigenous Africans. H.G. Wells and others have suggested a pan-Dravidian or pan-African culture of interconnected ideas, trade and commerce that stretched from the south of India, across Egypt and Nubia to the west coast of Africa."

This is during what is supposed to be the mythic-membership period, maybe earlier. The Sphinx has the face of a man. A black man.

Industrial societies in general have already brought us close to extinction as a species and have also made great advances toward the annihilation of our global ecosystem. The United States, which has historically been the leader in technological innovations and no doubt congruently militaristic developments has also by far promoted slavery more than any other nation (Muir, 2001). Environmentalism and general altruism or enlightenment are contiguous with each other in my opinion. An individual's or society's lack of consciousness is directly reflected in the amount of destruction caused by them to their natural environment. For these reasons I will address various attempts to promote white, patriarchal hegemony, including the "cyclic" vs. "accumulative" consciousness method, the written word vs. spoken word method, patriarchy vs. supposed matriarchy, and so forth in this section. Underlying all of the truths concerning indigenous cultures, ancient and contemporary, is a highly metaphysically influenced and sophisticated regard for ecology. I have already addressed the genius of traditional African socio-politics and given numerous paramount references to accounts of their economic and other substratas of genius. Here I will concentrate on a number of broad subjects, including how historical material developments by blacks reflect their traditional or ancestral views of nature and the place of humans in nature.

The mother is the theme of early childhood. Piaget is probably the most extensive child psychologist in history. In child psychology we have whole other stratas of the study of human development, the complexity of which can be likened to that of brain anatomy. Thus to look at the assimulative process involved from a phenomenological perspective would be something of a futuristic task. It is generally recognized that the growth of the infant occurs with the mother as the central focus. There has been a premature parallel drawn between this stage and early hominids. The latest date given by any modern, noted anthropologist for the origin of *homo sapiens sapiens* is 100,000 B.C. The *homo erectus*, 1.5 million B.C. already had a cerebral cortex, which is responsible for most neural processing. The *homo heidelbergensis* had a larger brain and appeared no later than 500,000 B.C. It understood full-fledged aerodynamics. The spears and other projectile weapons that it made were far from anything an average child could design. It systematically used the ores of rocks and the hardest, most efficient parts of trees to meet its purposes. A basic list of the functions of the right and left hemispheres of the brain in *homo sapiens sapiens* goes as follows:

Left Hemisphere	Right Hemisphere
Temporal	Spatial
Verbal memory	Memory of shapes
Analytic	Perception of wholes
Arithmetic	Geometric
Sequential motor coordination	Schemata body image
Spoken and written	Face recognition
language	Prosody and non-verbal communication
Cognitive, neutral	Affective, emotional
Introspective	Environmentally oriented
Reflexive	Impulsive

Homo sapiens sapiens, from the beginning, had all of the above listed brain functions, so "verbal-membership" began long before the neolithic period. In paleolithic art we have a vast vocabulary of techniques. There are depictions of three-dimensional perspective, which, as any art major knows, denotes geometric thought. This is the prerequisite for the most refined representational art. Commonly, the figures portrayed were anatomically correct and exquisitely animated, which has led many art historians to compare paleolithic art to the work of painters such as Vermeer. But these early *homo sapiens sapiens* did not only paint and sculpt representational art. They produced various styles of abstract and minimalist art, a broad vocabulary. Especially from a global perspective. Often they mixed styles, a representational animal with an abstract-expressionist mane, or minimalist figures surrounded by a diversity of linguistic-looking abstract designs, strangely dispersed. Wilber points out the fact that these images sometimes overlapped. He says that this denotes an inability to perceive the difference between subject and object. Figures did overlap in many of these paintings, but probably not for any exceptionally superstitious reasons. Actually this work resembles that of Carlos Alfonso or Jose Bedia, two contemporary geniuses from Cuba who make fortunes from their work. Wilber says that while most paintings were of animals, most sculptures were of fertility goddesses. In societies where the hunter is important enough to where animals and hunting were the most popular themes women would not have been altogether dominant. The fact that ten statues of fertility goddesses were found in a single cave does not mean that these people were matriarchal either. Actually there is no evidence that paleolithic people were matriarchal or patriarchal. Nor is there evidence, according to most neurologists, that their brain structures were inferior to ours. Latent depictions of goddesses are not, as Wilber claims, sufficient evidence that these people were matriarchal. There were plenty of depictions of gods also.

There is no conclusive evidence that the evolution of early hominids is parallel to child development. Physical dominance is the deciding factor of social hierarchies prior to the influence of fourth chakra altruism, not only with apes, but with all early hominids.

On one hand, developments themselves are not the only available indications of the intelligence necessary to acquire those developments. This is where structural anthropology, founded by Claude Levi-Strauss, comes in as the singular means to date of deciding equivalents among comparatively ectopic scientific modes and developments. On the other hand there has simply been a lot of academic and other forms of stratification. Europeans have always believed that, as Feuerstein put it, "The production of noise (e.g., jumping crackers, rattles, drums, hand clapping) belong to the ritual of all primitives who, like children, delight in acoustics, which can intensify, through the rhythmical element, to the point of ecstasy." There is much that we don't know about the brain anatomy of prehistoric people. The neanderthal had a larger brain-case than ours, but apparently it never got the hang of projectile weapons—which is commonly thought to be the reason it went extinct. It took a while for *homo sapiens sapiens* to cultivate different skills, agriculture and so on. It was difficult for them to overcome the elements. For tens of thousands of years there was trial and error regarding what foods to eat, how to build shelters, how to hunt, which medicines could be derived from which sources. There were incredible migrations, which were often the result of social disputes. There was the ice age, in which much evidence of these people's ways of life was undoubtedly lost.

Toward the end of the last ice age, maybe even closer to the beginning, people started to establish civilizations: technology, science and medicine. Carl Waldman in the *Atlas of the North American Indian* writes, "Increasing archeological evidence has pushed the estimated date for human arrival in North America further and further back, from about 10,000 B.C. to 50,000 B.C., perhaps even earlier, although there is still no consensus among scholars."

Around this time, when people began to establish the first cities, with farms and storehouses, hunting became less important. Women had always taken care of the children. They were able to farm as well as men. These first cities were, in this sense, the products of women. This was the beginning of civilization. Nicholas Mann in *His Story* suggests that words such as monogamy probably did not exist before that time, that men became more controlling of women and their patrilineages. Also during this period cities were probably so sparse that when different tribes did meet each other, one of them had traveled too far to want to war with the other. A lot of trading took place, as anthropologists of the later twentieth century have brilliantly shown. In the Americas a lot of trading at this time required latitudinal travel, which meant having to wear different clothes in different climates and so on. This was a significant challenge. Despite this the Mayans, a "cyclic" civilization, invented positional notation, which all higher math is based on.

Cyclic and Accumulative Societies

Another way that scholars have tried to confine every civilization before 2500 B.C. to pre-monotheism is by blowing their cyclic rituals out of proportion. This has far-reaching implications. It would mean that they had a weaker sense of self-identity, that they thought less about the future and the relation between what they did and where they were going. In terms of psychology the repercussions of this notion are profound. Wilber calls matriarchal thought-processes "cyclic" and patriarchal thought-processes "accumulative."

The accumulation of consciousness itself follows a spiral pattern. In other words, progress up the hierarchal ladder of consciousness is itself cyclic. Jung's model of spiral evolution is not entirely accurate, but it is valuable on many counts, and can, for the most part, be readily used as complimentary to the ladder paradigm. While Wilber, in *Eye to Eye*, claims that Jung was subject to ptf-2, elevationism, I do not agree. On the whole Jung's work was not defined well enough to be a metaphysic in the complete sense. His work was full of metaphysical elements, but it was not a complete metaphysic. His spiral format, unlike Michael Washburn's, did not involve a descent from or repression of egoic consciousness. Somewhat frustratingly, Jung obscurely but nevertheless legitimately acknowledged the necessity of explicating the "collective unconscious" into consciousness. He said, in works such as *Man and His Symbols* (1964), that the explicated collective unconscious was "perhaps more important" than its unexplicated version. So, he left some of the ultimate phenomenological questions unanswered, but he distinctly hinted at their correct answers.

At the same time, because of the less than optimal means—the collective unconscious—by which he arrived at a considerable degree of phenomenological conclusions, much of his terminology, references and lack of the latter were misleading. The term "depth psychology," for instance, can, upon first inspection, seem to connote a disregard of consciousness in favor of the unconscious. One reason that he used this term is that his prime area of study was the unconscious, rather than how phenomenological modes of consciousness function. He was ever in search of expressions of the unconscious. He analyzed what emerged from people's unconscious psyches far more than he theorized, or was capable of theorizing, about modes of purely phenomenological consciousness. We must understand that these aspects of the unconscious, once perceived by the physiologically conscious mind are no longer forms of unconsciousness. They are, at this point, consciousness. Therefore, when Jung spoke of depth psychology and probing the unconscious, what he effectually meant was explicating the unconscious (including the collective unconscious) into physiological consciousness. The means by which he did this and thought about it basically constitute an obscure, incomplete and occasionally inaccurate version of phenomenology or the ladder paradigm.

So, while Jung did not present a complete metaphysic, he did not exactly confuse the collective unconscious with the transrational either (ptf-2). More precisely, he obscurely suggested that the collective unconscious could not be differentiated from the transrational and likewise contradicted himself by stating that the explicated collective unconscious (which is, in relatively crude terms, transrational) is "perhaps more important" than the unexplicated version. He accuratetely said that with this explication "something new" is created.

Washburn, in *The Ego and the Dynamic Ground: A Transpersonal Theory of Human Development* (1995), has an entirely different version of the spiral paradigm. He is aware that it is not identical to Jung's. What he is not aware of is that he essentially presents an empty pseudo exoskeleton of Jung's spiral format. Unlike Jung, Washburn attributes the entire ego to a repression of the "Dynamic Ground." He describes the ego as originating in as the reconciliation of the infantile oedipal complex, but does not give any legitimate explanation of how the oedipal complex originates without an ego. Also he has an ungrounded version of a "dialectic" between his "mental-egoic pole" and his "Non-egoic, physicodynamic pole." The latter includes the "Dynamic Ground," which is the biggest problem. The Dynamic Ground, for whatever might be otherwise functional about it, cannot constitute a polarity. Jung did not consider his collective unconscious to be a polarity. Jung explained the collective unconscious as being outside of the psyche, and thus outside of the poles of the conscious and unconscious mind. Washburn's idea of a dialect between the ego and the Dynamic Ground has absolutely nothing in common with actual Hegelian dialectics. Dialectics can only exist between polarities. The Dynamic Ground, as Washburn describes it, is not polarized. If the ego were, as Washburn claims, primarily the result of a repression of anything transdualistic, there is no way that it could be valuable. Ptf-2 is exemplified by Washburn.

If Wilber understood these vital differences between the spiral paradigms of Jung and Washburn he would be better able to defend his work against Washburn. One of Wilber's major shortcomings is that, while he is a genius at fifth chakra theory, he is not particularly great when it comes to reading between the less obvious phenomenological lines. The way he has underestimated Jung (a fourth chakra figure who was exceptionally influenced by the fifth chakra), though largely due to the obscurity inherent in Jung's work, is the same way that he has failed to detect numerous historical fifth chakra and upper fourth chakra individuals. The decipherment of metaphysical qualities, in the context of poetry, will be one of the main subjects of the final section.

Jung understood the necessity of the explication of individual consciousness and many universal truths concerning this process. But boundaries between different levels of eros are still largely obscure in his work, as are the distinctions between different modes and functions of eros. The reason is that Jung, rather than founding his ideas on an authentic, phenomenological ontology, founded them by way of his observation of the collective unconscious. The collective unconscious was a loop-hole through which Jung arrived at many phenomeno-logical conclusions. But, because his basis was not really ontological, his episte-mology was prone to distortions. His idea of the conscious mind resembles the symbolic aspect of phenomenology. His idea of the unconscious resembles the sensory aspect of phenomenology. And his collective unconscious resembles the spirit aspect of phenomenology. But none of his ideas were based on phe-nomenological ontology, which is why there were consistent inaccuracies in his work at large.

The ladder paradigm, as Wilber defines it, transcends Jung's inaccuracies and his obscurities. It is, from the ground up, infinitely more applicable in terms of understanding the psyche. I believe that if Wilber comes to terms with considerably more advanced means of supporting his ladder paradigm he will have conquered his patriarchal, Eurocentric misconceptions.

Unfortunately, even some of the rare scholars who do have a basic under-standing of the ladder paradigm tend to overlook the more subtle issues regard-ing latent regression. This is marked by typically masculine forms of repression. In other words, if ones pursuit of higher rungs on the ladder is overly concep-tual there is a tendency to lose touch with the unconscious counterpart, body-mind integration and so on, which generally results in repression and neurosis. The third chakra version of this is exemplified by much of historical Europe, with its repression of rhythm, bright colors, the naked body, body-mind inte-gration and so forth, all basic elements which are essential to socio-political harmony. Expressions which increase harmony in balanced societies and exalt disharmony in unbalanced societies. Nelson believes that the ladder and spi-ral paradigms can work together. Washburn has not ruled out the possibility. Without the employment of cyclic rituals, ie., most nonindustrial societies, accumulation in the phenomenological sense is not possible.

What we must do is integrate the useful aspects latent in nonindustrial soci-eties (which often had superior languages, body-mind integration, taxonomi-cal, sociological and other systems) with the useful aspects of modern societies (which have made vast contributions in various areas of art and science). The creation myths that were prevalent when Europeans discovered other civiliza-tions are the only creation myths those civilizations knew. They were rarely matriarchal. So, already we have matriarchy ascribed to people who clearly were not matriarchal. Because of this Wilber claims that many nonindustrial societies, even many existent today, have not differentiated various aspects of their religions and social structures in terms of gender. This is an example of the absurd lengths that Eurocentrists have gone to in order to support their views.

In hermeneutic philosophy there are three disciplines: the spoken word, interpretation and translation (from foreign tongues). Of these three the spoken word is considered to be the most important. The fact that these people thought cyclically is obviously not due to any lack of an understanding of linear time. And a simple acknowledgment of linear time as we know it today was all that the written word intrinsically necessitated. If these people were primitive they are not much less primitive today. Mayans still live in the same thatched-roof houses that they lived in during the pre-classical era. Native Americans still pray to the Great Spirit.

Wilber proposes that typhonic people were at level two and that the exceptional ones, the shamans, could reach level five. So, these people who collectively revered their shamans, fifth level personalities, were supposedly only second level, on the average. Wilber even calls them "sub-human." He considers them to be marked by impulsiveness—along with mythic-membership people. What he describes as typhonic consciousness is holographic, as distinguished from mandalic consciousness. (He describes the holographic paradigm skillfully in *Eye to Eye* and other works.) The two are superficially similar in that they both expand potentially endlessly from every direction and area. In the holographic paradigm, however, there is no real ontology, nor is there a sound epistemology to speak of. The idea is that the physical world, like a giant piece of holographic film, shows its seamless entirety through any and every fragment of itself. With this paradigm there is no epistemological direction. It does not explain the need for ethical direction or hierarchy. It states (though most who have adopted it are unconscious of this fact) that there is no ontological problem. By doing this it does not provide a basis for rational differentiation in general. Mandalic consciousness also expresses that the sum of the parts exists in each of their divisions, but it does so by referring to an ontological basis, from which epistemological, ethical and hierarchal direction are derived.

The holographic paradigm is a peculiar, latent manifestation of fourth chakra consciousness. It is usually well-intended, but not necessarily responsible, nor is it completely rational. Wilber does not call typhonic or mythic-membership consciousness mandalic, but I think that the overall qualities of the consciousness that he describes in regard to these levels and of those that compose the holographic paradigm are, for all means and purposes, identical. And the holographic paradigm is basically a product of fourth chakra consciousness. Mandalic consciousness (phenomenology and other forms of metaphysics) is, as I have repeatedly stated, the embodiment of fifth chakra consciousness. This is completely rational as distinguished from the comparatively rudimentary reasoning of the third and fourth chakras.

We of modern societies tend to commit our shamans to mental health, as have the bulk of historical European societies. Ancient indigenous people who exalted their shamans (these shamans could usually be male or female, equally) are supposedly third level. Wilber draws direct links between typhonic and mythic membership people and modern indigenous people.

On one side of the spectrum we have impulsiveness. On the other we have repression. Neither is ultimately preferable to the other. Both lead either nowhere or to regression.

At the least we can say that European repression was far more excessive than impulsiveness was in other regions. Also what we are dealing with is primarily fourth chakra "cyclic" societies vs. primarily third chakra "accumulative" societies. Rather, most nonindustrial societies were both accumulative and cyclic; they viewed time both sequentially and as perpetually regenerating itself. These two principles do not contradict each other, they compliment each other. The reason Europeans lost sight of cyclic time is that they became too obsessed with material technology and wealth, basically, and with documenting their conquests and developments. Everything became, as Wilber has said, "a chronicle of the ego's accomplishments." Cyclic consciousness is spiritual, if not necessarily metaphysical. It expresses an awareness of the oneness of death and birth. Accumulative and cyclic consciousness are only mutually exclusive where an individual or society is overly consumed by its own ego (exclusively accumulative) or in instances of unconscious nihilism (exclusively cyclic or accumulative). Cyclic consciousness does not necessarily entail a denial of material, sequential reality. It is based on the importance of the life force (or magara). This life force is beyond the ego, it sees the perpetual death and rebirth of the ego. While it can be given due consideration by an individual or society, this does not necessarily mean that the individual or society lacks acknowledgement of the sensory and symbolic aspects of the psyche. Thereby it does not necessarily mean that the society lacks a strong self-sense or understanding of the existential nature of accumulative time. When Wilber speaks of "accumulative" consciousness he is largely referring to the appearance of works by Greeks such as Herodotus and Homer. There are many intermingled factors to consider. There were fourth and even fifth chakra influences in European culture. But the accumulative aspects were dominantly third chakra.

Levi-Strauss' contributions in the way of understanding what he called *la pensee sauvage* or "concrete logic" are manifold. Here I will list some of them.

He acknowledged that in the popular indigenous view most art was intentionally symbolic, that for these people, "the model always exceeds its image." Likewise, far from attributing this to superstition, he said that the European tradition of representational art was typically a product of trying to create (normally unconsciously) an effigy of the object represented. He recognized that to these indigenous people time was both linear and non-linear, whereas to Europeans it was only linear. There were European philosophers as far back as the Greeks who knew about non-linear time, but almost no one understood them. Levi-Strauss showed that the mythological, totemic, sociological ecological, taxonomical and exchange systems of nonindustrial people were entirely functional and far-sighted. They had an infrastructure that, while supporting cyclic rituals, were adaptable to changes in populace and so forth. These were all parts of encoded, interconnected systems. These schemas were, by any human standards, nothing less than encyclopedic. They generally did not use the written word to document any of it. They memorized it without the written word. In other words, they were obsessed with the functional interrelatedness of everything in nature. Levi-Strauss said that at the heart of *la pensee sauvage* was "bricolage," a "form of combinatorial logic." This was how these systems were designed. Bricolage is, in Levi-Strauss' words, "a way of thinking which must imply that if you don't understand everything, you don't understand anything." He discovered that Amerindian myths were similar in structure to musical forms such as fugues and sonatas. Tribal societies used to pass around a shell called the Kula Ring. It would reach dozens of tribes, moving either clockwise or counterclockwise. This was to insure harmony among these people. Their cyclic rituals were intrinsically accumulative. They simply were not as possessive in terms of what they invented as many European civilizations have been.

It was not that these people had no concept of long-term progress or that they lived strictly in the moment. Their emphasis was to renew everything constantly. They knew that insuring the psychological health of the people was a full-time job. Most European societies were completely negligent to the inner psychological landscape and natural interconnectedness that these people were almost exclusively interested in. Levi-Strauss' list of discoveries in structural anthropology continues extensively.

Wilber concedes that Levi-Strauss is possibly the greatest anthropologist in history, yet he does not adequately regard structural anthropology. In this right he arrives at an ethnologically reductionistic view. This is unfortunate, since in virtually every other area Wilber has had a singular part in aiding the triumph of integrative philosophy over reductionism.

As soon as we have excessive militaristic fervor (supposing that all militaristic fervor is not excessive) we have gone through the passage to ecological annihilation. With the invention of the crusader castles, most of which were built in the eleventh century, and guns, which originated in the eleventh century we had an infinitely greater destructive potential than previously known. It was akin to militaristic fervor in general, prior militaristic fervor included, and this point should be judicially examined. Another context is that with these militaristic inventions destructive militaristic potential in general escalated infinitely. This would have been true even if the first to own these innovations had not set out to conquer other empires. With these original exaltations of militaristic power the nuclear arms race, really, had virtually already begun.

It is nearly impossible to undo such inventions, let alone the historical implementation of them which continues to run its course. It comes down to which factions of the human race have been historically more aggressive. Aggression and intelligence are never necessarily contiguous with each other. Aggression and consciousness are never contiguous with each other under any circumstances. Somehow it is thought by numerous current scholars and authors of various fields, from anthropology to psychology, that historical aggression was a byproduct of respective evolutionary growths of consciousness. It is a tragic misconception which continues to appear in books to this day. Beyond this, intelligence itself is not necessarily contiguous with consciousness.

We must realize that the only probable way that our current ecological, nuclear arms and similar crises, could have been avoided is by having never caused the original escalation in militaristic competitiveness. One faction builds castles, another faction, if allowed and not far-sighted enough, builds castles in response. The same applies for guns and militaristic advancements in general. As soon as there is an excessive militaristic fervor, more precisely, as soon as militaristic advancements become the priority of a society, that society has passed through the gate of an improbable return to harmony. Without much further effort in the same direction, it has effectually brought the entire human race with it.

Approximately eleven square miles of world's rainforests are destroyed each day. At least three species disappear each hour (*Nature Conservancy*, September/October 2000). In the United States one in every seven people are malnourished. Every time a space shuttle is launched three tons of aluminum dust goes into the atmosphere. Global warming, landfill, nuclear power plants: all of these were the virtually inevitable consequences of our original departure from indigenous life.

To understand the psyche requires a culture's full attention. As soon as guns were invented or crusader castles or sophisticated catapults, it was plain to see that, if implemented, they would evoke attempts by other factions to develop more destructive militaristic utilities.

Hominids have walked the earth with a cerebral cortex for 1.5 million years. *Homo sapiens sapiens* have lived since at least 100,000 B.C. Hominids have crafted fairly sophisticated projectile weapons since the *homo heidelbergensis*. Europeans did not invent guns until the eleventh century A.D. Nine hundred years later would mark the release of atomic energy. For 100,000 years humans did not have guns, castles or similar militaristic inventions. Then, in a span of nine hundred years we went from the first singular escalation of militaristic advancements in the history of humanity to the release of atomic energy. Now, fifty years after the release of atomic energy we have virtually destroyed ourselves and our ecosystem. My point is that the lauded materialistic developments of Europe are what started the snowball. It simply was not like, *Oh, great snowball; we'll have to be careful to not let it get out of hand.* On the contrary, the snowball, despite demonstrating a certain evil intelligence, did not in any way represent an evolutionary growth in consciousness. There are plenty of harmful actions that a person or society could plot that would require considerable intelligence, but that intelligence would not represent a form of consciousness per se, if consciousness leads to verticle evolution.

To say that there was ever an evolutionary ascent that had as a byproduct an increase in violence (whether the latter was necessary or not) promotes the misconception that consciousness can, in itself, entail violence. Consciousness and violence are mutually exclusive. Neither an individual nor a culture can ever be more conscious than an individual or culture that is less violent than itself. This is a singular tenet of the supernal philosophy.

If we try to refute this point, at best, we contribute to a pseudo-justification of violent behavior while making those who are the martyrs seem less conscious than those who afflict the violence. From there others can further exaggerate the same idea with its previous subscriber(s) as their valid support.

It is true that with the increase of abstract thought that the frontal lobe entailed there was contiguously an increase in anxiety and potential violence. But this, rather than justifying human violence, simply meant that humans could direct their new cerebral resources in a positive, worldcentric direction or in a destructive, selfcentric direction.

The leader(s) of a society and the status quo of that society directly reflect each other. A society with selfcentric leaders is comprised of generally selfcentric members. A society with worldcentric leaders is comprised of generally worldcentric members. A minority of shortsighted individuals cannot normally defeat a majority of relatively enlightened individuals.

If Utopians existed they would probably not need written language. If they were living in a hot region they would probably dress scantly because they would not be ashamed of their bodies. They would have much better body-mind integration than most people in industrial societies have. They would not have much material technology because they would be immersed in psychological and cosmological matters at large, and their occupation with these subjects would manifest as a proliferation of views that would seem to us, as industrialized people, in our technological and dissociated arrogance, to be peculiar. It would probably manifest as completely dislocated expressions in art, like an almost complete lack of mimesis and a fervent immersion in the principals surrounding classical cubism and other indigenous forms of art that Europeans and people of European extraction would not rediscover until the twentieth century, in many mediums, including music, dance, painting, sculpture and literature.

Material Developments

Let us address science, technology and the written word as they pertain to African cultural development. About 11 million African slaves were brought to the Americas between 1451 and 1870. This was the first displacement. There was a second that coincided with the Emancipation Proclamation in 1863. This event was contiguous with various forms of new socio-political stratification, the long-term result of which was ultimately the movement of blacks to project housing. (I do not have the space to go into this here. The most comprehensive source on this that I know of is Jeanine Canty's *Cultural Ecopsychology: Issues of Displacement and the Urban African American Community* (2000).) Despite this, between 1826 and 1905 an estimated 7,488 blacks in the United States had graduated from colleges and professional schools. By 1925 at least twenty-one blacks had earned doctoral degrees in the United States. By 1942, at least forty-three.

In 1913 Henry Edwin Baker published a book titled *The Negro Inventor* which revealed some four-hundred previously un-publicly benounced black inventors. In 1895 the U.S Patent Office advertised its first exclusive exhibit of the inventions of blacks. Many of these were not small inventions. There was Benjamin Banneker (the first striking clock with all parts made in the United States, the prediction of the solar eclipse of 1789), Norbert Rillieux (steam engine work and steam engine economy that became popular among scientific circles across Europe, 1830), Augustus Jackson (ice cream, 1832), Lewis Latimer (first cost-efficient method for producing carbon filaments for electric lights, many important innovations in the development of electric lighting), Granville T. Woods (Improved telephone transmitter, numerous patents dealing with railway telegraph systems and electric railways), Andrew J. Beard (coupling device for rail road cars, 1895), Garrett A. Morgan (three-way automatic traffic signal, 1912), Frederick McKinley Jones (first practical refrigeration system for trucks and railroad cars), George R. Carruthers (NASA Exceptional Scientific Achievement Award for work on an ultraviolet camera), Walter McAfee (involved in first radar contact with the moon), to name a few. There have been at least six black astronauts, including Frederick Drew Gregory who was the first black space shuttle commander.

Although indigenous people have generally not had written language Wande Abimbola (1994) says that poems in the Yoruba oral tradition number as many as 204,800. If these were transcribed they would comprise one of the most extensive literary texts ever. Richard Spears (1991) states that unpublished folktales in West Africa often number two-hundred from a single tribe and that for Yoruba-speaking people at least five-thousand are estimated.

If we have to think in terms of consciousness ultimately being connoted by things like pianos, guns and airplanes, sure, Europeans and Asians take the cake. Blacks, of course, are more misunderstood than any other ethnicity. There have been many racists in the history of white academics: Voltaire, Hume, Kant, even Hegel. According to Jahn (1961) Levy-Bruhl was the first to introduce a supposedly comprehensive theory of the "prelogicism" of indigenous people. He renounced this view before his death, "The logical structure of the human mind is the same in all men."

Jung, who for most of his life catered to Eurocentric notions, also learned to appreciate the contributions of indigenous people as documented in one of the two last books that he wrote, *Memories, Dreams Reflections* (The other being *Man and His Symbols*) and in Laurens van der Post's definitive biography, *Jung and the Story of Our Time*.
Here are some excerpts from *Memories, Dreams, Reflections*:

> "There for the first time I had the good fortune to talk with a non-European, that is, a non-white. He was a chief of the Taos pueblos,

an intelligent man between the ages of forty and fifty. His name was
Ochiwiay Biano (Mountain Lake). I was able to talk with him as I
have rarely been able to talk with a European.... with this Indian,
the vessel floated freely on deep, alien seas.... 'See,' Ochwiay Biano
said, 'how cruel the whites look. Their lips are thin, their noses sharp,
their faces furrowed and distorted by folds. Their eyes have a staring
expression; they are always seeking something. What are they seeking? The whites always want something; they are always uneasy and
restless.' ... 'They say they think with their heads,' he replied. 'Why of
course. What do you think with?' I asked him in surprise. 'We think
here,' he said, indicating his heart.' ... For the first time in my life,
so it seemed to me, someone had drawn for me a picture of the real
white man.... And out of this mist, image upon image detached itself:
first Roman legions smashing into the cities of Gaul, and the keenly
incised features of Julius Caesar, Scipio Africanus, and Pompey. I saw
the Roman eagle on the North Sea and on the banks of the White
Nile. Then I saw St. Augustine transmitting the Christian creed to the
Britons on the tips of Roman lances, and Charlemagnes most glori-
ous forced conversions of the heathen; then the pillaging and mur-
dering bands of the Crusading armies. With a secret stab I realized
the hollowness of that old romanticism about the Crusades. Then
followed Columbus, Cortes, and other conquistadors who with fire,
sword, torture, and Christianity came down upon even these remote
pueblos dreaming peacefully in the sun, their Father.... The Pueblo
Indians are unusually closemouthed, and in matters of their religion
absolutely inaccessible.... the religions of civilized nations today are
all accessible; their sacraments have long ago ceased to be mysteries.
Here, however, the air was filled with a secret known to all the com-
municants, but to which whites could gain no access.... I feel sure
that the Pueblos as an individual community will continue to exist as
long as their mysteries are not desecrated.... If I had hit on something
essential, he remained silent or gave an evasive reply, but with all the
signs of profound emotion; frequently tears would fill his eyes. Their
religious conceptions are not theories to them (which, indeed, would
have to be very curious theories to evoke tears from a man), but facts,
as important and moving as the corresponding external realities....
I then realized on what the 'dignity,' the tranquil composure of the
individual Indian, was founded. It springs from his being a son of
the sun; his life is cosmologically meaningful, for he helps the father

and preserver of all life in his daily rise and descent. If we set against this our own self-justifications, the meaning of our own lives as it is formulated by our reason, we cannot help but see our poverty. Out of sheer envy we are obliged to smile at the Indians' naiveté and to plume ourselves on our cleverness; for otherwise we would discover how impoverished and down at the heals we are. Knowledge does not enrich us; it removes us more and more from the mythic world in which we were once at home by right of birth.... That man feels capable of formulating valid replies to the over-powering influence of God, and that he can render back something which is essential even to God, induces pride, for it raises the human individual to the dignity of a metaphysical factor.... Such a man is in the fullest sense of the word in his proper place."

Africa: "The feeling-tone of this curious experience accompanied me through-out my whole journey through savage Africa. I can recall only one other such recognition of the immemorially known. That was when I first observed a para-psychological phenomenon, together with my former chief, professor Eugen Bleuler.... All in all, Negroes proved to be excellent judges of character.... They could imitate with astounding accuracy the manner of expression, the gestures, the gaites of people, thus to all intents and purposes, slipping into their skins.... It was a paradisal world."

The first tribe in Africa that he documents are the Maasai. These are all excerpts about the Maasai:

"As in Southern Europe, men speak to men, women to women.... Their dignity and naturalness flow from their function in the econ-omy; they are intensely active business partners. The concept of equal rights for women is the product of an age in which such partnership has lost its meaning. Primitive society is regulated by an unconscious egoism and altruism; both attitudes are widely given their due. This unconscious order breaks up at once if any disturbance ensues which has to be remedied by a conscious act.... Gibroat—the son of a chief, charming and distinguished in manners ... My hostess was plainly and unproblematically the embodiment of stability ... What goes on in the interior of these 'simple' souls is not conscious, is there-fore unknown, and we can only deduce it from comparative evidence of 'advanced' European differentiation.... Thousands of miles lay

between me and Europe, mother of all demons. The demons could
not reach me here—there were no telegrams, no telephone calls, no
letters, no visitors. My liberated psychic forces poured blissfully back
to the primeval expanses.... In general the people asserted that the
Creator had made everything good and beautiful. He was beyond
good and evil. He was m'zuri, that is, beautiful, and everything he
did was m'zuri.... [after sunset] The optimistic philosophy gave way
to fear of ghosts and magical practices intended to secure protection
from evil. Without any inner contradiction the optimism returned
at dawn.... the laibon's words and his sprinkling of milk unite the
opposites; he simultaneously sacrifices these two principles, which
are of equal power and significance ... The important thing, however, is the moment when, with the typical suddenness of the tropics,
the first ray of light shoots forth like an arrow and night passes into
life-filled light.... It is a maternal mystery, this primordial darkness.
That is why the sun's birth in the morning strikes the natives as so
overwhelmingly meaningful.... The moment in which light comes
is God. That moment brings redemption, release.... The longing for
light is the longing for consciousness."

It is obvious that a monotheistic, cosmologically differentiative solar logos
appears throughout all of the Pueblo and Maasai passages. Then, on the last
page of the Africa section Jung contradicts himself, "The myth of Horus is the
age-old story of the newly risen divine light. It is a myth which must have been
told after human culture—that is, consciousness—had for the first time released
men from the darkness of prehistoric times. Thus the journey from the heart of
Africa to Egypt became, for me, a kind of drama of the birth of light."

Their empirical differentiation is embodied in their vast accomplishments in
all areas, with the two exceptions of militarism and the written word. The written word, since its conception, has been primarily a means of control, not a
means of enlightenment. I, as a writer, would be better off without the written
word. With the written word it was possible to more easily manipulate people,
to lie, to stratify masses. With the written word an emperor could send letters
announcing a law within a specified radius, and anyone within that radius who
did not obey the law could be punished as the emperor saw fit.

   If indigenous peoples had been as war oriented as the European conquestors
there would have been larger city-states among them. There were hiways that
stretched for hundreds of miles in Africa (DuBois 1915, Bynum 1999). There

were long trade routes in most indigenous lands, and the natives traveled those routes, for the most part, in peace. The way city-states develop is this: one faction develops better weapons than another, which enables the former to conquer the latter, take their land and, especially if they have a written language, stratify their people. Afterwards the faction that developed the superior weaponry is stronger than before and all the more conditioned to make further militaristic advancements. If they have a written language they can broadcast their brutality, which tends to intimidate their prospective enemies. A genuine domino effect. That is how city-states emerge. When one tribe conquers another the result, of course, tends to be a larger tribe. Larger tribes can more easily conquer smaller tribes. That was not particularly common. If it were there would simply have been larger city-states among those indigenous people, and, of course, those city-states would have no longer been indigenous.

Every sensible person knows what a perfect democracy is, an equal voice for everyone, the collective acknowledgement of individual talents. Every sensible person knows the difference between malice and consideration, between harmony and brutality. Absurd militaristic advancements have not exactly, as popular academia suggests, furthered our understanding of harmony and perfect democracy. It is a matter of being able to meet scholars on their own ground. If a means of measurement is proposed we must be able to use the same means in order to illustrate our point. If scholars present uninformed or misinformed empirical comparisons to support their claims, we must be able to present correct empirical comparisons to support our claims. If they suggest metaphysical evidence, we must be able to counter with metaphysical evidence. There is an objective map. Evolved people lived long before our subjective words. It is our responsibility to discover how they lived (through whatever academic means are available) and to present the means of our knowledge to the world.

Another argument that has been raised in support of the patriarchal dissociation that was exalted (not born) with the emergence of the Bronze Age is that previous cultures were in some ways more brutal, namely, with their notorious ritual sacrifices. Once slaves had been commodified to the extent they were with the influence of Europeans, it hardly made any sense to continue sacrificial rituals. Obviously there was no intent on the part of the slave traders to sacrifice themselves, and they also had no reason to sacrifice their commodities. Supplementing this fact was the escalation of war, which made soldiers another form of commodity. In war and in the incomparable degree of slave trading themselves there were plenty of sacrifices. Given, they were not ritual.

In contrast to Europeans who massacred anyone who did not call the Creator by the name of Christ, most indigenous peoples were more confident in their religious, philosophical and psychological views. This was evidenced by the fact that the outer structures of their religions were so easily adaptable while the essence of their religions was so easily kept from the views of their European conquestors. (Their religions all had the same universal essence.)

They regarded spiritual issues dialectically. They understood that a name is not the object that it identifies, but that knowing the specific objects that names do identify is necessary to communication. So, whereas many modern psychologists harbor the misconception that indigenous societies were generally predifferentiative, indigenous peoples usually differentiated not only empirically, but, as I have shown, dialectically (or metaphysically) as well.

It seems evident that many nonindustrial people were at a somewhat mandalic version of the fourth chakra. Many paleolithic societies might have been as well. We should not arrive at premature conclusions about prehistory based on limited information. Wilber concedes in some detail that even paleolithic societies had shamans and that these shamans had psychic abilities. Clearly anyone with a religious inclination is able to distinguish between their minds and their bodies. They depicted shrines, deities and shamanic activities. They buried their dead. Buried remnants of early hominids have been found adorned with flowers and animal skulls. There was a spiritual concept of forces of dark and light. This would have been impossible if they had been unable to differentiate between their minds and bodies. Basically, they did not confuse thoughts with flesh in the typical sense. It is more likely that they were person, that the typhon did not often have a sense of body-mind integration. Later "cyclic" people, however, in some cases accumulated greater calendars than the Roman calendar that we use today. In some cases they accumulated more advanced verbal languages. Indeed, they accumulated superior understandings of eco-systems. Their prominent civilized accomplishments did not coincide with their thorough consideration for nature without considerable intelligence.

Animals do not rise up and from the earliest traces of abstract, discursive intelligence automatically understand the complete interconnectedness of nature. This is invariably a reflection of world-centric consciousness, no lower than the upper fourth chakra. It was not the result of an inability to differentiate oneself from the rest of nature (holographic). It came from the ability to see the relation between oneself and the rest of nature (mandalic).

Wilber knows perfectly well that because most environmentalists are pre-mandalic they fall short of understanding the components necessary to a complete ecological perspective. They do not understand phenomenology—which is basic to any metaphysics including mathematical, environmental, astrological and so on, nor do they understand bricolage. And bricolage, as I will show, is also metaphysical. Imagine the world before anything existed. Then, out of the ineffable Oneness, geometric spheres of time and space expanding endlessly from every direction. These spheres constituted sound, smell, taste, texture, and every other quality manifest in nature. There were original expressions of each of these qualities, which constituted the first family. All of these qualities were related to each other. They shared the same origin. Then this family began to multiply, creating more families. Each of these new families shared the same origins, respectively. In this sense everything in nature is systematically related. Objective causes, in themselves, produce both objective and subjective effects, according to what places these causes have in the natural world. Whether a particular sound is produced by one source or another does not, in itself, matter. That sound produces a predetermined outcome. Rather the possibilities made manifest by one occurrence are not the same as those produced by a different event. This is according to the same principles of cause and effect described in phenomenology. An outcome has an objective source or sources, which is in accord with phenomenological ontology. This existential fact is the basis of mandalic consciousness. While, in some cases, a certain expression is not an accurate reflection of the source from which it comes, it does have the same effect, in itself, as it would if it came from any other source. This is grounded in the strictly phenomenological recognition of the roles of objectivity and subjectivity. (You do not learn this in Jungian psychology.)

Nonindustrial people were not only commonly experts at this level of thought, they understood systems of interrelation on levels that were comparable to the later innovations of phenomenological hermeneutic philosophers. Namely, the understanding of the role of history, how contexts changed. Forms of bricolage were usually, as I mentioned earlier, geared toward adaptability to latent circumstances, such as droughts, changes in populace and so forth.

One of the simplest ways to illustrate bricolage is metonymically. Levi-Strauss has done this in reference to names of pet dogs, pet birds, race horses and so on. This form of metonymic systemization is observable cross-culturally and cross-linguistically. There is the mythological naming of planets and so on. In European thought these associations have not been given much consideration. There are, however, metaphysically important reasons for the existence of metonymical patterns. Reasons that have little to do with anything other than metaphysics. The singular principle behind such patterns is ontological, the fact that all subjective states depend on objective circumstances. Objective and subjective in strictly and necessarily metaphysical terms. For instance, I prefer the word enormous to its synonym tremendous. This is because I associate enormous with words like elephant (which sounds similar and means a large animal), emu (sounds similar and is a large bird), immense (sounds similar and is a synonym of enormous) and so on, whereas I associate the word tremendous with tremble (a verb that is associate with small things), trim (rhymes with slim, means to make something smaller), tram (which is like a smaller version of a train) and so on.

Likewise we can see that where exceptional attunement to the fifth chakra is found there is generally a more laconic and hermeneutically capable use of words. Examples would include Piaget, Greenberg, Einstein, all of the most metaphysical writers.

So, a full explanation of bricolage actually necessitates references to phenomenology. The fact that an understanding of phenomenology has been absent in Europe would explain why Europeans rarely understand bricolage. Since fifth chakra reasoning is the only potentially complete form of reasoning I consider pedanticism to be the antonym of phenomenology. At the end of the nineteenth century Hegel was supposedly in fashion, but we can see from the course that has run that few of these professed fans of Hegel understood his work. This is a perfect example of European pedanticism. All of the rediscoveries that Europeans have made in art and science which nonindustrial societies regarded as common knowledge. We have tried to substitute these with empirical modes and ideologies. It has only led to self-destruction. This is the kind of pedantic quality I am referring to, where intelligence is bereft of substance and geared only to make oneself look superior, whether by embellishing meaningless statements or by pretending to understand something substantial that one does not really understand.

Nonindustrial people were mostly concerned with stability and harmony. To them it was ridiculous to think of progress without first having stability. Also there accomplishments, architectural and so on, where evidence enough that they were not as militaristic as Europeans. Anasazi architecture was equal in beauty, durability and function to any European architecture of the same period—with the arguable exception of gothic cathedrals, which appeared in the twelfth century. But Anasazi architecture, the wooden architecture of the North West Plains and so on—while Equal, for all means and purposes, to any European architecture of those periods—did not reflect a comparable militaristic interest. Likewise, ancient Africans were probably the best iron smiths in the world. Some tribes made superb chain-male, but they never went as far as

Europeans in crafting it as armor. In Benin they made exquisite armor out of coral. They could have easily made suits of metal armor like those of Europe, but they didn't.

Bricolage, while metaphysical, was also in perfect accord with Jung's principle of synchronicity. It, in fact, embodies a more refined understanding of synchronicity. Jung caught glimpses of metaphysics, much the way that the Greeks and Neoplatonists did. Extremely few Jungian psychologists, especially in modern sociological circumstances, would be capable of expertise at the science of bricolage, including Jung himself.

So, the ideas of progress and linear time of these nonindustrial people were commonly thoroughly equal to those of Europeans. They were always acquiring new information, which was largely used to maintain harmony between themselves and other tribes.

War and slavery was common among non-Europeans, but not in any manner comparable to how it existed because of Europe.

The identities of nonindustrial people were largely represented by totems. One of the prime functions of these totems, as I have said, was to maintain harmony between tribes and within tribes. This way each tribe knew the character of the others. Individuality was generally, collectively exalted in tribal societies. A strong ego cannot be attributed to third chakra consciousness at all. Tyranny and the self-identity of a people are mutually exclusive, in any context. At the third chakra we have people who are comparable to animals, except that they use politically superior brains to achieve their animalistic goals. There was simply less territorialism in pre-industrial societies. Levi-Strauss discovered many of the means by which they maintained harmony rather than causing tyranny. He pointed out that these people were rarely competitive. That was one of the reasons they were so ritualistic. They often used rituals instead of sports, because rituals brought people together rather than singling out victors and losers. Commonly, when they did play sports, the sports were designed in a manner that both sides would come out equal. For instance, they would play the game until both sides had even scores. This, the Kula Ring, their advanced languages. The Wichita language, as one example, is arguably both more articulate and efficient than English and other European languages. Richard Rudgley gives what is possibly the most definitive account of nonindustrial surgery in *The Lost Civilizations of the Stone Age*. He presents several cases, described in detail by anthropologists, of tribal doctors performing complex surgeries, sometimes better than European surgeons were able to at the respective times. None of this is in accord with the idea that these people tended to be primitive.

One way to measure ego definition is by way of evidence of an unwavering discernment of truth. Where we have wide-spread false accounts of obvious states and events we can see that the source which they are attributed to (the respective culture) does not know itself. Phenomenologically, individuality cannot be composed of falsities. If we are trying to describe the true individual and the degree to which it knows itself we cannot confuse arrogance with divine principle. To do so would promote dialectical obscurities. This being the case, Wilber casts a distorted account of self-sense by claiming that it is, in any context, personified by the likes of Hitler, who, if he had possessed any sense of who he was, would not have tried to cover up the true identities of other people.

With the rise of industry, many indigenous cultures have dissipated. Those that remain are not as fortified in their ancient ways because their young are influenced by white people and by the media. Africans outside of Africa do not generally have a known history. The only known history that they have is the history of their lineages since their ancestors were brought to wherever their respective regions were. This was more true in the beginning of the European conquest. As late as the twentieth century Europeans imposed laws against the utilization of traditional technology and medical procedures by indigenous people. In the fifteen hundreds most texts were burned wherever Europeans went, because anyone who was not a Christian was thought to be corrupt. We can read in text books that the bronze casts of Benin are induplicable even today. Then we try to find out when the casts originated, and the texts say, *We're not sure. We think they go back to about the time that the Portugese got there.* Virtually the only creation myths we have accounts of from any of these people are monotheistic and ultimately tie in with panentheism. They prayed to fire because fire is holonic. They prayed to their arrows because their arrows were holonic. They identified with animal spirits, not because they confused animals with humans, but because on the basic level, everything under God is equal. There were other reasons too.

In dreams animals can appear as good omens. This is a generally recognized fact in modern psychology. To these people—and this surpasses even holonic theory, but is contiguous with it—there was a thin distinction between dreams (which are only unconscious physiologically) and the waking state. It is also generally recognized in psychology that events during the waking state affect our dreams, and that the reverse is also true. Somehow in transpersonal theory the idea is held that dreams are a higher level of consciousness than is the normal waking state. But dreams simply reflect what is happening in the waking state. Dreams are nothing other than symbolic interpretations of the objective events which occur during physiological consciousness. It is common for psychologists to speak of dreams this way, but they do it only semi-consciously. I will go into this more in the next section. The point here is that—much like the Picasso syndrome, where Picasso is a genius when he depicts what are otherwise "primitive" images—animals can be identified with in dreams, dragons can be used in Buddhism, but when ancient indigenous people identified with animal spirits they are thought to have been confusing subject with object.

Van Gogh lived a tragic life and died tragically because he was not understood during his time. Europeans would not understand Picasso for another fifty years. At that time he would be regarded as one of the greatest geniuses in the history of art for painting images that Africans and other ancient people sculpted hundreds—in some cases, thousands—of years earlier. When it comes from Africa it's called "primitive" (often even by current art historians). When a European paints the same thing in the middle of the nineteen hundreds it's called genius.

It is a commonly known fact that the art of a culture corresponds directly to that culture's science. The keen awareness, alone, of the fact that one cannot duplicate objects, as expressed prolifically by nonindustrial societies, lends itself to the idea that at least a significant percent of these people were aware of ontological reality, which does not seem to have been volubly expressed by any historical European philosopher until Amo in the eighteenth century (Nwala (Ed.), 1990). (After Amo, it does not seem to have been volubly expressed again by any historical European until Hegel, *who was born about sixty-seven years after Amo and whose basic metaphysical tenets non-lumpen proletariats throughout the First World are still by-and-large violently against.*)

I will go a step further by saying that I agree with Plato's stance about premature artists. One might be able to produce hypnotic art. This artist generally has a spectacular charisma. It is because of this that if the same artist is at a pre-rational level they can be a profound threat to civilization. To have an exceptional degree of influence over people and to, at once, express false concepts is dangerous to everyone. This personality would only have pull with a pre-rational society. In conjunction, pre-rational societies do not have adequate veneration for higher reasoning (especially fifth chakra reasoning). What this means is that not only does such an artist lead people to exaggerate the value of the pre-rational, he also leads people to disrespect higher reasoning.

The first guns (as crude as they were) were invented in the eleventh century. By the fourteen hundreds they were considerably improved upon. It was in the fifteen hundreds that most of the major invasions began, although the original Roman conquest of North Africa spanned from 220 B.C. to 46 A.D. The clothes of most indigenous people outside of Europe were no less sophisticated than those of Europeans. There was comparable wooden and clay architecture in most other regions. There were a number of early stone buildings in various parts of Africa (other than Egypt), such as Nubia, the Cape of Good Hope, Zimbabwe and the Sahara. There were the sophisticated houses of the North West Coast Plains Indians, the Anasazi cliff dwellings (some which contained more than two-hundred rooms) and so forth. The first European palaces were built in Crete, in 2000 B.C. But the Cheops pyramid at Giza was built by Africans a thousand years earlier. The first first paved streets in Rome were in 170 B.C. By this time stone architecture had begun to flourish in parts of Europe and the Near East. Gothic architecture and most the crusader castles were erected in the twelfth century. Given even the progress accomplished by Europeans, there were, arguably reasons that this happened: Climate, natural resources, and so on. Europe was cold compared to Africa and most regions where Native Americans lived. In cold geographies straight trees grow, whole forests full, mostly, of tall, straight trees. In the upper west coast of North America you find a climate similar to that of Norway. The development of architecture in both of these regions is similar. This is not that big of a point, but it does bear some significance. In particularly hot regions, why would people want excessive, ornate stone architecture and roads? Unless they were influenced by architectural traditions from cold regions. Or, unless they were particularly militaristic. There are plenty of detailed anthropological accounts of the fact that the surgical techniques of many pre-industrial people were on a par with those of Europeans, at least as far back as the nineteenth century. We're talking about naked people who performed flawless caesarean sections in the nineteen hundreds using roots and leaves and no sutures. Any linguist can tell you that many of these people had some of the most advanced languages known to date. Linguists emerged from non-European or Near-Eastern societies. They were first noticed by settlers in the seventeen hundreds, after their people had been overthrown and scholarly interactions were more often possible. Then there are factors such as Europeans building houses in California, where earthquakes are common, that do not withstand earthquakes, whereas the natives there had already lived in pueblos, which are architecturally perfect for withstanding earthquakes. The first stone tools were found in Africa in 2.4 million B.C. The first harps and flutes were found in Egypt in 4000 B.C. (Japanese people were the first to invent boats and pottery, in 10,000 B.C.) The list goes on. In the final analysis, pre-industrial societies were not, on the whole, that far behind

Europe. For the most part, the only way that Europe was more functionally advanced was militaristically: fortresses, armor, guns and other weapons. This had nothing to do with superior consciousness, or any necessary evolutionary step. There was, of course, also the written word. But this is only implementation, not superior literary ability. The written word, as Levi-Strauss has said, was largely a tool for conquest. It heightens politics, which are not always honest. We do not know conclusively who first domesticated horses. It is likely that they were first domesticated in Central Asia. Some say that it spread from there into Europe through Troy several hundred years B.C.

In *Up From Eden* Wilber describes the European dissociation fairly accurately. His mistake was largely that he overlooked the vast evidence of the metaphysically superior rationale of nonindustrial societies. Panentheism must come from at least fourth chakra sources, whether consciously or otherwise. Concern for the environment and an ability to establish harmonious societies are also evidence of fourth chakra consciousness. It is third chakra consciousness that is preoccupied with high-tech weapons, brutal conquests, and that—if not dealt with gracefully—results in corruption and denial of its own behavior. European standards of materialistic development are not necessary to the attainment of fourth, fifth or higher chakra consciousness. Rationalism is a necessary part of evolution. Hysteria, in the metaphysical sense, is not. Third chakra European history, far from being necessary to the attainment of goals we still have not reached, has been the consummate behavioral embodiment of hysteria. Generation upon generation, for at least 2,500 years doing everything in their power to defend nothing substantial against anything substantial. In many indigenous cultures there was the concept of the co-existence of linear and non-linear time. An empirical scientist will usually say that time is only linear. A new-age fanatic will usually say that time is only non-linear. In most exceptional cases, if asked to explain the co-existence of both, these people become visibly nervous. We must take into account such psychological factors, those that Levi-Strauss has pointed out, those that are in accord with Jung's innovations and those that have bearing on current phenomenological psychology. The only other option is racism. It is not necessary to create a dissension among the ranks, since all ethnicities—including Europeans—have contributed more-less equal bodies of altruistic genius. These bodies of artistic and scientific accomplishment have also been unique to each ethnicity.

Non-Europeans have rightly been hailed by a growing number of ecopsychologists, anthropologists and ethnologists as being ecologically mindful. These functions were not superficial. There are no superficial functions in nature. Humans are the only beings capable of being unnatural. This can happen at any chakra, as supreme liberation is beyond the chakras. Indigenous people prior to colonial influence had encyclopedic memories, which they used primarily for evolved ecological and socio-political purposes. We cannot presume that societies are generally inferior due to their lack of militaristic development. We must look to profounder factors. We cannot continue in modern psychology or any other science to view Europeans as the most conscious ethnicity. Based on the intrinsic hierarchal idea that I support as much as Wilber, this would mean that white people should enjoy privileges that no other ethnicity should have. In other words, the whole equality issue would be a joke.

Indigenous people outside of Europe and the Near East had successfully married the concept of growth with the concept of perpetual rebirth. After 100,000 years of human evolution—especially since, as every anthropologist knows, *homo sapiens sapiens* came from Africa—this should not be difficult to accept. It is third chakra consciousness that is potentially pre-occupied with the overemphasis of material gain. Since many of these indigenous people had more sophisticated languages than the European settlers and, in several cases, written languages it is ridiculous to think that they were not as literarily intelligent. Since they produced a far more psychologically broad vocabulary of art and full-scale "religious" wars, by European standards, were practically unheard of among them, it is not particularly insightful to conclude that they were intellectually incapable of producing more destructive weapons.

Just as the behavior of any creature can be good or bad (in the phenomenological sense), each stage of chakra development can be dealt with benevolently or otherwise. Beings at any stage can be patient and tolerant or they can be violent and overbearing. What we have in European history is a violent interest in third chakra conquests. This was undeniably the result of applying reason only as far as it suited selfcentric pursuits. The only social interests entailed were political, not humanitarian. There were more enlightened influences, but primarily it was the conquest of vain glory. The virtual obliteration of the eco-system cannot come from anything higher than third chakra consciousness. There is no way to rationalize away this fact. Other indigenous people were not all destined to become what Europe has been. Although Wilber concedes that the supposed transformation from the mythic-membership level to the solar-ego level also entailed an unnecessary dissociation and deformation he does not describe in detail what the alternative would have been. Usually he refers to the transformation as it supposedly occurred as necessary.

They try to support Eurocentrism with monotheism. That doesn't work because most societies had monotheism when they were discovered. Few of them had written languages. This is to say most of them had monotheism before they had written languages. Also, other cultures didn't have versions of Christ. If Jesus had lived among most of these people, they would have considered him to be a great shaman. As much as we might rationalize this point, its simple profundity cannot be dismissed.

There is the popular misconception that an adult who avoids, say, hairy men because of repeated trauma caused by a hairy man while they were a child, is guilty of the pre-differentiation (usually subconsciously) between the individual who caused the trauma and other hairy men. An idea originally introduced by Freud. It is also popularly paralleled with the supposed pre-differentiation of typhonic people. There is rarely such a pre-differentiation either in modern people or in typhons, which were also *homo sapiens sapiens*. A person may be weary of hairy men because of a rational association. If they were traumatized by a hairy man as a child, it is rational to be wary of hairy men in general until the person has gathered sufficient evidence that not all hairy men are liable to traumatize them. An actual confusion of subject with object as often described only occurs in the most severe cases of psychosis. Then it is usually due to an emotional incapacity to differentiate between identical and similar subjects. The discernment of such individuals is stifled and they use metaphors as if the metaphors are real. It is a kind of hysteria which occurs when the individual is emotionally overwhelmed. They literally do not have the emotional energy to regard the sources of or solutions to their traumas systematically, so they opt for a desperate amalgamation of literal and metaphorical associative references.

In less severe cases a person might even confuse a person who looks similar to the person who traumatized them with the person who actually traumatized them, which is not due to pre-differentiation either. It is due simply to the fact that trauma makes people appropriately cautious. Their views of the limits of possibility are rationally expanded. Likewise children from the ages of two or three are capable of differentiating cartoons from real people. Aspects of pre-differentiation in infants are generally likened to the inability to discern what is edible from what is not edible. It is more lack of experience than of mental capacity that such non-distinctions are attributed to.

The assimilatory processes of infants are complex enough on the levels that Piaget addressed. To apply these to chakra development complicates the matter much further. With infants there is the emergence of an entire psyche, in all of its aspects. They are able to distinguish, to the degree that they are informed, the differences between genders. They know the difference between an animal and a representation of that animal. All of the information that they attain from

the earliest ages is attained according to a natural system which is firstly cognitive but contiguously syllogistic. Both are necessary to the development of children and *homo sapiens sapiens*. There is no pre-differentiation in either except
in cases where one is emotionally incapable of differentiation, and, of course, in
individuals with mental disabilities.

There is also the type of association which consists of not wanting to be
reminded of a certain trauma. If a person was abducted in a blue volkswagon
that person might not like blue volkswagons because they remind the individual of their trauma. They do not confuse one blue volkswagon with all others.
Rather they (consciously or otherwise) associate blue volkwagons with the origin of their trauma, which they do not want to relive, even in memory.[5]

An extraordinary imagination does not generally hinder the faculty of object
constancy either. Hyper-active imaginations are usually the result of an exceptional capacity for object constancy, to the extent that the networks of object
constancy described to such individuals by the people in their environments—
as accurate as they may be—do not supply adequate mental stimulation. This
type of imagination cannot be repressed, as it is contiguous with normal modes
of object constancy. Repression of this type of imagination only amounts to
prolonged regression. Exceptionally imaginative processes are a means of
acquiring systems of object constancy which are suited to the individual's intellectual capacity. If one does not exercise their inherent imagination their cognitive, syllogistic processes (object constancy) are arrested. Healthy assessments
of literal, consensual reality do not take place without ample regard for their
metaphorical counterparts.

This is in allegiance with both the spiral and ladder developmental paradigms. The ladder paradigm is, in itself, more cut and dry. It represents the
scale on which final assessments are reciprocated. In order to progress on the
ladder, however, one must follow the spiral paradigm as well. There is always an
interplay between concepts and the unconscious.

We are supposedly to believe that, while second chakra (typhonic) individuals
collectively nominated sixth chakra individuals to be the priests of their societies, third chakra modern individuals do not venerate modern individuals.
This is what Wilber and others propose to be the historical facts. I subscribe

---

5   The two best books on post-traumatic stress disorder are Peter Levine's *Waking
the Tiger* and Judith Herman's *Trauma and Recovery*, in that order. There is also
Donald Kalsched's apparently pioneering work on schizophrenia and early childhood trauma specifically, titled *The Inner World of Trauma: Archetypal Defenses of
the Personal Spirit*.

to Nelson's view of the sixth chakra rather than Wilber's, to begin with. But, aside from this, Wilber has prodigiously described the relation between different levels of eros. They are all, in a sense, incompatable with one another. This is to say that where we have the co-existence of two different individuals on two different levels of eros there is an inevitable forfeit of eros assigned to one or the other individuals. This forfeit can manifest as either regression or evolution. If it is an evolutionary forfeit, the transition can either be benevolent or abrupt. In the case of transition to a higher level of eros, it is more of an integration of the former level than a forfeit. The word forfeit does apply, however, since the transition always consists of a dramatic shift in orientation.

The point is that different levels of eros are, in a certain respect, mutually exclusive. When they interact harmoniously there are only transitions from lower levels to higher levels. If there is an individual at the fourth level, however, and another at the third level, as Wilber describes, what ensues is the horizontal maintenance of each of these levels by the respective individuals. A mutually supportive relation between these two levels would require an extraordinary degree of mutual cooperation. For this reason it does not make any sense that a second chakra society and a sixth chakra shaman could mutually support each other. As we see in modern societies, the acceptance of fifth chakra individuals by those at the third chakra is difficult enough.

Tibetan Buddhist culture is a good example. We have patriarchs who are often fifth chakra. The people who revere them are usually fourth chakra, occasionally fifth. The 14th Dalai Lama has a large following now in many parts of the globe. This following is usually fourth chakra. People at the third chakra, which is most first-world people, sometimes have an insincere interest in Buddhism. The first humanitarian chakra is the fourth.

If second chakra societies did regard the value of the sixth chakra, or even fourth chakra, it would be exceptional. We are not talking about an arbitrary reverence. It would entail the sacrifice of second chakra consciousness, in which case further evolution would occur rapidly, given the most basic consideration for lower chakra necessities. At the second chakra a relatively distinct separate self-sense does not yet exist, which makes Wilber's model, in itself, at least two steps removed from the truth. So, let's say that we have a fourth chakra society nominating sixth chakra shamans. This would connote a remarkably strong fourth chakra ego on the part of the status-quo of that society. In other words the ego definition of a society can be measured by observing the relations between individuals of varying levels of eros within that society. Where we have harmonious interactions between individuals of different levels of chakra consciousness we have healthy ego definition. Where these harmonious interactions are absent we have weak egos. It is not due to an exceptional ego on Hitler's part that he was able to attract a large following. It was because the Germans and the rest of the Axis had an inadequate sense of self-identity.

Modern psychologists—for all of their genius—have gone as far as to view the unspeakable acts of European history as having been ultimately beneficial to the human race. As though these conquests were inevitable.

It is my belief that third chakra consciousness was inherent in all human beings, ie., *homo sapiens sapiens*, from the beginning. Bonobos (a member of the pan genus, like chimpanzees) are able to communicate verbally in the strictest sense. They can follow commands involving complete sentences that they have not previously heard. They are not capable of any of a number of skills that pre-verbal human children are capable of. There is a long list of similar differences between the developmental patterns of early hominids and those of modern human children. Third chakra consciousness is a human given. How much that consciousness is emphasized by a particular culture is another matter.

We can take, for example, the fact that age thirteen is when females begin menstruation and males begin to ejaculate. These functions correspond to the second chakra. What we must be sensitive to, however, is that with infants we have the emergence of an entire human psyche. Limited functions at different stages cannot be so readily relegated to chakra limitations. The development of a child is part genetic, part familial and part sociological. All of these determine the consciousness of the individual. At the earliest stages the main immediate influence is the mother. But the male infant does not normally emulate his mother throughout the early stages of the developmental process. On the contrary, to the degree that his father comes into the picture, the male child identifies with those masculine qualities. This connotes a differentiation at the early stages of childhood.

Feminism is and always has been basically segregated. Stella Tamang, a Nepalese indigenous women's rights leader, actually does apparently speak for at least the vast majority of indigenous women's rights leaders when she says, "The international women's movement does not represent indigenous women."

Beyond this, prominent indigenous, black and other feminists—i.e., Davis, Jordan, Lorde, hooks, Collins, Oyewumi, etc.—are virtually unanimous in saying that mainstream and popular feminist academia is generally a mere abstract extension of standard colonialist and neocolonialist academia.

Scholarship on female genital mutilation (FGM) in Africa is generally racist. *Virtually all infibulation—which is basically the most severe type of FGM—is practiced by Muslims. The term "pharaonic circumcision" as a synonym for* infibulation *is a racist misgnomer.* (The ancient Egyptians practiced partial clitoridectomies and male circumcision exclusively (Abdalla, 1982).) *Et al.*

My best hypothesis is that infibulation was introduced by Egyptian Muslims—at least a large percentage of whom might have been black and Africoid—in northern Sudan sometime around the eleventh century A.D. and from there was rapidly introduced to Mali (which is often referred to as the Muslim capital of West Africa, because of the historical Mansa's—black Muslim Emperors—of Mali, Mansa Musa, etc.), and so on.

In terms of religious demography throughout Africa, the severity and frequency of FGM corresponds with remarkable consistency to the concentration of Islamic members of the populace in a given geography. Likewise, geographically, in terms of the practice of infibulation versus less severe forms of FGM, the latter evidently sort of surround the former like bone around marrow or like an egg-white around a yolk.

It is as Okome (Oyewumi (Ed.), 2003) says, "Western feminist discourse on female circumcision continues the colonial tradition of the enlightened westerner attempting to reform the 'backward' populations of Africa."

The best feminist anthology that I know of is *African Women and Feminism*, edited by Oyewumi (2003).

When the actual concept of an afterlife and spirituality enters the picture, we already have gender distinctions. These gender distinctions, like all gender distinctions, are built in biologically and are basically constant throughout the evolution of all animals. The spiritual aspect, to the degree that it genuinely exists, has nothing to do with these gender distinctions, per se. The suggestion that the concept of something that created all of nature (monotheism) can arise prior to the ability to differentiate basic functional differences between matriarchy and patriarchy is absurd.

As I have said, in terms of hierarchies, we have two possible modes: physical dominance (first chakra through the early stages of the fourth) and metaphysical designation (upper fourth chakra and higher). Bonobos demonstrate a considerable verbal capacity (as do dolphins). Other animals demonstrate simpler verbal capacities. None of these animals have a cerebral cortex. Hominids have been walking the earth with a cerebral cortex for 1.5 million years. Popular transpersonal psychologists actually claim that there were human societies that functioned without abilities that are latent even among animals.

Sadly, the fact that indigenous people were not as carried away by the third chakra made them susceptible to being misinterpreted as inferior to those who were. Consideration for ecosystems, for example, can be superficially adopted by people whose behavior is based on third chakra consciousness for political and/or sociological reasons. It can be adopted, sincerely or otherwise, by those at the fourth chakra. But its prime rational basis is the fifth chakra. What we can see from this is that where there is perfectly evident third chakra development coupled with more metaphysically far-sighted cultural values there is, somehow, a fifth chakra influence. Laing knew this. Bynum knows this. Feuerstein and Nelson do not realize how thoroughly they support this simply by giving such conclusive accounts of kundalini yoga.

In industrial societies people generally dislike fifth chakra figures until those fifth chakra figures become celebrities. Then the attitude is, *Well, it's O.K. that these people are powerful, because they're not human, they're celebrities.* This does not constitute a sincere reverence for fifth chakra consciousness. The same sociological factor probably applied, to varying extents, among nonindustrial people. Regardless, the point is that there was this influence. Evidence of this is abundant. Most likely, considering the extent and scope of the indications of fifth chakra attunement, the status-quos of most of these civilizations were at least fourth chakra. Shamans would not be able to function to their full capacity if the people catering to them were lower than fourth chakra. This would likewise account for the remarkable secrecy surrounding their religions. This also applies to divination techniques, which are of a particularly fifth chakra nature. Most new agers do not understand the fifth chakra. At the same time Wilber does not understand the principle of synchronicity as well as Jung, who coined the term, did.

While the works of prominent feminists of color are consistently brilliant, they often do not offer much in the way of insights about historical or existent matrifocal or matrilineal societies.

There are some—though very few—brilliant prominent white feminist authors—i.e., Karen Horney, Allison Jagar and Marianne Williamson. But they tend to not give us much insight about matrifocal or matrilineal societies either.

I do not have the space here to go into anthropological, etc. dimensions of females' roles in indigenous societies. As I have said, *neither Stone's "matriarchal" societies nor Gimbutas' "matristic" societies are really anything like any traditional matrifocal or matrilineal society in Africa or anywhere else that I know of.* (I've looked at a pretty good amount of indigenous artifacts, and I haven't seen any depictions of sacred orgies with women in the center of them or anything like that, etc.)

The three best sources on matrifocal and matrilineal societies that I know of are Nancy Tanner's essay *Matrifocality in Indonesia and Africa and Among Black Americans* and Peggy R. Sanday's essay *Female Status and the Public Domain* (Rosaldo and Lamphere (Eds.), 1974). And *Cultural Survival Quarterly*, which publishes the voices of many progressive indigenous women from around the globe.

Individuation, according to Jung, who coined the term, involves the conscious and unconscious mind equally, for both sexes. He was very interested in medieval alchemy, in which—as in the Chinese yin and yang dichotomy—male is equated with the sun and female is equated with the moon. But despite this he says explicitly that *neither sex is more solar or lunar than the other.*

Because individuation—which can be seen as an objectively accurate sense and perception of oneself—is equally necessary to both sexes and, by definition, involves the conscious mind and the unconscious equally, neither sex is more conscious or unconscious than the other.

Davis (1998) is right when she says in regard to mainstream and popular feminism, "The abstract negation of 'femininity' is embraced; attempts are made to demonstrate that women can be as non-emotional, reality-affirming and dominating as men are alleged to be. The model, however, is usually a concealed 'masculine' one."

Meanwhile scholars like Davis, Jordan, Lorde, hooks, Collins, Oyewumi, Okome, *et al.* are saying that females must reclaim their own agency. They are authentically fighting for gender balance and, with a centuries-old plenitude of reason, expressing outrage at the *violently pseudo-progressive solipsism expressed collectively by white feminists and proponents of mainstream and popular feminism in general.*

Mainstream feminists must get past the paradigm that says that males versus females are by nature more competitive, differentiative, hierarchical, agentic, etc. (The equation that both Eurocentric patriarchs and Eurocentric feminists very often subscribe to is: male = "doing," female = "being".) and start paying a decent amount of attention to indigenous societies, and so on.

It should be clear that females' sexual power basically corresponds to males' combative power. This has to do with existential biological realities, etc.

Mainstream and popular feminists, by and large, seem to only admit that males are generally combatively dominant—due to their osteology, muscle mass, etc.—in reference to the subjects of rape and sexual assault. As progressive authors of feminism—i.e., Oyewumi—have stated, part of what we generally find in mainstream and popular feminism is a dissociation of the soma—or corporeal body—in general, to say nothing of the male and female somas specifically.

As I have said, metaphysically, the soma = the personal unconscious (or relatively objective self) = feeling = the anima or animus, etc. And likewise, because it is an expression of the *other* (other than the subjective self), its integration corresponds, at the fifth chakra, to consciousness of the ontology.

Let us now look at what happened when people were taken from their supposed "primitive" societies and brought to other regions. Phillis Wheatley, a poet from the seventeen hundreds who was brought as a slave from west Africa as a child, mastered Greek and Latin on her own. There were many similar cases. Either she was the equivalent of Einstein to her people or her people were not relatively primitive. We can rest assured that the latter was true. The materialistic simplicity of these people corresponded to their psychological sophistication.

In sports, athletes such as Jesse Owens, Muhammad Ali and Michael Jordan were not champions because of their physical strength alone. Even in non-contact sports intuition is the main factor. Every great scientist has had an athletic intuition, an ability to move from one idea to another without necessarily calculating the wind in between. The same is true for sports. A sprinter must be able to demodulate the psychological factors that allow him to rise above his competition. In contact sports the same applies, except that during the game this intuition must be more spontaneous as well.

I believe that jazz is esoterically a fifth chakra art form. Improvisation is a central element of jazz. Only a minute number of classical European composers considered improvisation to be an integral part of music. Jazz musicians have proved to be as capable of creating masterpieces as classical composers ever were. There are jazz musicians who are every bit as skilled as Mozart. Pianists like Art Tatum, Sun Ra and Bud Powell literally sound like ten people playing. Robert Johnson could play the guitar as if it were a piano. The modern jazz pianist Marcus Roberts performed an unsurpassed rendition of Mozart's Requiem, conducted by Bobby McFarren. There was jazz fusion, heralded by Miles Davis. Quincy Jones and others have said that Miles Davis revolutionized jazz five times. There was the funk, pioneered and mastered by George Clinton. Sun Ra created a type of space age jazz, often using electronic instruments such as the moog synthesizer. He is said to have written over a thousand compositions and to have produced at least 240 albums. He mastered the piano by the time he was eleven, a year after he began playing. Rahsaan Roland Kirk was known to play six wind instruments at once (and he played them as well as anyone ever played a single wind instrument). Jazz musicians such as Leon Parker and Wynton Marseilles continue to innovate to this day. Most classical virtuosos concentrate on playing compositions written hundreds of years earlier with relatively little variation. Sun Ra's orchestra, which was called the Arkestra, often consisted of twenty to thirty members. Clinton's orchestra also had musicians numbering in the twenties. In addition, musicians like Sun Ra and Clinton were working with concepts and combinations of instruments that were previously unfounded.

Wilber says that jazz does not reach higher than the fourth chakra, whereas classical music reaches the fifth and sixth. He should listen to Sun Ra's *Jazz in Silhouette* or *Monorails and Satellites* or Leon Parker's *Above and Below*.

Most of the great pioneers of jazz: Monk, Ellington, Roach, and dozens of others were from the beginning and are still formidable metaphysical philosophers. This is documented in books. We can also speak with modern jazz musicians and find this out straight from the source.

To assess the overall historical and current intelligence of any ethnicity we must take into account more than the empirical details, such as the development of weapons and empirical literature. We must consider, as much as possible, mandalic influences. Those that are based on the same reasoning Wilber, Laing and others have done so much to promote. Not only for ethnological and feminist reasons, but for ecological reasons and metaphysical reasons in general.

CHAPTER FOUR

Poetry

In chapter one I addressed the Negritude poets and the surrealist poetry of Europe, South America, etc. and stated my hypothesis that surrealist literature is most developed in Mexico and the West Indies. However a lot of exquisite—remarkably metaphysically tuned—surrealist literature has also come out of countries like Cuba and Argentina. And of course a lot of great, highly symbolic and inventive modern poetry has been produced throughout Africa by poets like Ken Saro-Wiwa, Wole Soyinka, Kojo Laing, Dennis Brutus, Chenjerai Hove, et al.

In modern African poetry there is a tendency toward traditionalism, a lot of mention of ancestors and elders, etc. African literature, like the literature of pretty much any other geography, has developed in its own ways and embodies certain unique qualities.

As Tanure Ojadaide and Tijan M. Sallah explain in their introduction to *The New African Poetry: An Anthology* (Ojaide, T. and Sallah, T.M. (Eds.), 1999), the present generation of African poets is considered to be the third.

The first generation of African poets, so to speak, wrote during the colonial period and at least largely expressed Greco-Roman and Victorian values. The second generation began sometime around the late fifties and included Wole Soyinka, Dennis Brutus, Kofi Awoonor, Okot p'Bitek, etc. The third and current generation continues the tradition of the second generation and traditions of ancient indigenous Africa, but it has proven to be prolific; it expresses great virtuosity, inventiveness and metaphysical consciousness. Third generation poets include Niyi Osundare, Jared Angira, Chenjerai Hove, Kojo Laing, etc. (There is a lot of overlap between second and third generation African poets. In other words, some of the third generation poets were prominent around the time that the major second generation poets began to widely receive critical and public acclaim, and some of the major second generation poets are still writing today.)

Soyinka writes (1975), "One conspicuous quality of U Tam'si's poetry, in company with Rabearivelo's, Nortje's and others', is that it is structured within a conceptual tradition which embodies essentials of the metaphysics of the African world."

Both the second generation and the third generation African poets very often skillfully express pervasive aspects of ancient indigenous African metaphysical thought.

Here is an excerpt from a poem by the Nigerian poet Niyi Osundare titled *Excursion*:

> Past the depleted copper of harvested cornfields
> Past the leafy grove of ripening yams
> Past the groundnut's leguminous lilt
> in the orchestra of swinging furrows
> Past the bean which has a thousand children
> with antimony in each eye
>
> Past the gallant butterfly dallying from flower to flower
> Past the bee droning and dreaming in the hammock
> of fallowing farms
> Past the dung-beetle rolling in its forbidden ball
> Past soldier ants bootless in their lengthy columns
>
> Past the lake lying namelessly in the register
> of famous shrubs
> Past the duck which brailles liquid letters
> on its open face
> Past boulders and pebbles which answer the whisper
> of calling feet
> Past the quivering arrow of a noonward sun

Osundare uses a lot of symbolism in this poem: a bee in a hammock, a bean with a "thousand children with antimony in each eye," etc. Yet, as with dream symbolism, symbolism in literature and so on can only be interpreted so many ways. *In the final analysis, if this were not true there would be no discipline called hermeneutics.*

This excerpt is an example of metaphysically voluble—regardless of whether or not this metaphysical knowledge is being presented consciously—and articulate in general use of symbolism.

The "boulders and pebbles which answer the whisper/of calling feet," for example, could be reasonably interpreted to be a reference to the dialectical process. The "bean which has a thousand children/with antimony in each eye" could be a parent who has children who are gifted but who have to deal with a lot of internalized oppression. We can conjecture that because shrubs are dependent on lakes the lake should be "famous" and the shrubs should perhaps be "nameless". Osundare could say that the ants are "bootless" as though he is responding casually to the question, asked by an imperialist, "Are the ants wearing boots?" And so on.

The supernal philosophy can be confusing for people who are not familiar with it. For one thing we are using dialects. So, one word can have variable meanings, including its opposite. Throughout dialectical usages there are also potentially limitless mandalic dichotomies.

In order to understand advanced verbal expressions of the supernal philosophy one must decipher dialects. These dialects are often not presented in full. Often various dialects are used in a single poem. In a poem there might be only a few dialectical bones from a cow combined with the dialectical exoskeletons of blowfish and an arrangement of dialectical flowers, all decorating the coagulated swamp of a single metaphor. Poets often express dialects metaphorically and metaphors dialectically. A philosopher might use no more than one esoteric dialect throughout a chapter of a book. Poets often use numerous equally esoteric dialects throughout a single poem. They use dialects to bridge dialects. They use casual metaphors to convey vast metaphors of metaphysical direction.

It is a principle of the supernal philosophy that everything alive is new and thus unique. Likewise, what ever is not alive is redundant. Because of this the ground is always fertile for the talented metaphysical philosopher. Poets who understand this use poetry to cover as much of this ground as possible. They convey a level of acceleration that is natural to them, through the only possible verbal means other than mathematical references.

Poetry is a way for metaphysical philosophers to write their thoughts as they occur or as they appeal to the poet. This means that the expression of the supernal philosophy is often obscure to all but the most skilled metaphysical philosophers. There are good reasons for this. Firstly people should be able to express beauty in any form. There is no such thing as unethical beauty. Anything that is unethical cannot be beautiful. One can think of something unethical as "beautiful" subjectively, but in metaphysics we are also dealing with ontology (objectivity), which means that what we think is true and what is true are not always the same thing. Also, everyone needs a means of positive mental stimulation. Metaphysical poetry provides a type of mental stimulation that cannot be found in any other type of literature.

Metaphors are literary versions of symbols. Dream symbolism tends to be metaphysical because it is nothing other than a translation of the events that take place during the waking state. As Wilber has said, translation is a horizontal process. The consciousness that takes place in dreams, during physiological unconsciousness is not superior or inferior to the consciousness that takes place during the waking state. In the waking state events are equally metaphysical, objectively. Dreams are a more laconic translation of these same events. We can interpret events in the waking state or those from dreams in terms of equal degrees of metaphysics. The essential difference is that dreams are a more laconic expression of events in the waking state.

Europeans did not begin to adhere to surrealism (unless we count Heronymous Bosch) until after the dada movement and the first World War, with the appearance of Andre Breton, Max Ernst, Georgio De Chirico, Roberto Mati and others from various parts of Europe. These painters had their literary counterparts in poets such as Paul Eluard, Federico Garcia Lorca, Ramon Gomez De La Serna, Antonio Machado and others.

Surrealism, from the Greek *sur*, meaning *super*, was, from the beginning, associated with metaphysics in Europe. Many of the prominent figures of this renaissance were capable metaphysical philosophers. De Chirico's school of metaphysics in Italy had a large and inspired following. Even Salvador Dali was a brilliant metaphysical philosopher. He once said, "Truth and the philosopher's stone go hand in hand." Freud once psychoanalyzed Dali and came to the conclusion that Dali's consciousness and subconscious were the reverse of those of most people. In other words, according the most acclaimed psychiatrist of the time, Dali was conscious of what was supposed to be his subconscious mind while what was supposed to be his conscious mind was his subconscious. The early surrealist movement, as a whole, presented far too many challenges to the academics of their time. As a result absurdities such as Freud's diagnosis of Dali occurred.

The primary functional current of surrealism has always been that of a sort of spontaneous, unconscious vehicle from which the mysteries of ones emotions can be explicated into comprehensible logic. This is especially important in cases where ones unconsciousness is less accessible to themselves because that individual's consciousness is less accessible to themselves. In other words, cases where ones consciousness is particularly incongruent with that of the status-quo. While such an individual would, in better socio-politic circumstances, be more proportionately in tune with their unconscious and emotions than the status-quo is with their own—the fact that they must always battle for their own objective knowledge diminishes what would otherwise be a suitable and natural attunement to their unconsciousness. Surrealism is, above all, the mechanism with which such an individual can retrieve their own vital, unconscious messages.

Images or words might appear spontaneously. Those that inspire the individual can be investigated. In skilled hands they can be made visible to others by way of artistic or scientific reproduction. Surrealism is not limited to art, a point of this chapter which is of paramount importance. At first, one will perhaps aim only at explicating the unconscious image or thought without immediately deciphering its imminent meaning. Afterwards, one might give an elaborate dialectical interpretation of an image or a line of abstract poetry. Dali "resolved the metaphysics of De Chirico with pure mathematics."

Ancient examples of surrealism can be found from various geographies: a priest with mushrooms protruding from his shoulders, faces composed of human figures. What constitutes surrealism is anything that one would not see during normal waking consciousness. Naturic amalgams, mythological animals such as dragons, centaurs and Cyclops can be considered to represent surrealism. The most crisp definition we can apply to surrealism is anything that one would only see in dreams or similarly altered states of consciousness. In this sense mythology and metaphorical art tends to be surrealistic. Surrealism is the expression of metaphors in any medium.

The same type of metaphors are prominent in dreams. In hermeneutic philosophy and bricolage we learn that any symbol, whether it is literal or metaphorical, has a limited amount of correct interpretations that can be applied to it. This coincides with the emphasis of the influence of history in hermeneutic study and the science of bricolage. Any correct mode of interpretation depends on the context of the given subject matter, which is always a product of history, whether the states and events of history involved are empirical or metaphysical. Because of this language, whether literal or metaphorical, is as much a matter of limited available subjective interpretation as it is about the objective intentions of its usage.

Linguists, psychologists, new agers and others have offered numerous accounts of such modes of interpretation. This is to say, modes of finite possible interpretations of language. Usually they are not specifically aware of the hermeneutic implications of their endeavors. As an example let us say that one dreams that they have ten arms. Depending on the context, the message of the dream might be that the individual is executing extraordinary accomplishments. Or, in a different context, the message might have something to do with the number ten. The dream might even be a vicarious play on words. It could mean that one is in possession of ten destructive weapons or "arms."

One might dream that, looking in a mirror, they see the reflection of a sucker fish. They might interpret this to mean that they have been acting like a parasite. The dream might actually mean that they have been a "sucker" or a dupe. To interpret languages we must understand the contexts in which they are used. The context is part of the language.

We can interpret statements empirically, as Freud did, or we can interpret them metaphysically. Empirical statements can be interpreted metaphysically. Metaphysical statements cannot be interpreted empirically. It seems to be for this reason that there has always been a metaphysical tendency among surrealist artists. Dreams are a more laconic translation of events that take place during physiological consciousness. This is to say that surrealism is a more direct expression of ontological reality. Nothing is spoon-fed in surrealism. With surrealism we are supplied with the immediate contents of our unconscious. We can only volubly understand these contents through metaphysical means. Empiricism goes in circles because it is not ontological. Thus, when one is presented with inevitable collages of ontologically induced subjective states, they can either dismiss it as irrational, which is a way of ignoring it, or they can investigate it metaphysically. One can interpret dreams empirically to an extent. But, on one hand, such endeavors, as far as they go, tend to entail mistakes. Also, one cannot acquire a genuine overview of the general language of dreams without metaphysics. With laconicness comes invariably the penetration of linguistic dimensions in general. Thus surrealism, being the most laconic language of all, tends to confront one with existential and, likewise, metaphysical questions. At which point one can either investigate what does arise irrationally or they can tell themselves that the surreal depiction is completely irrational. The latter is due to a lack of metaphysical orientation and typically evokes in the observer a feeling of being unsettled. In the case of being compelled to decipher these unconscious messages, we find people who are generally, likewise, interested in metaphysics. Surrealism is a metaphysical threshold, which—when crossed—yields a more expansive degree of expression and inventiveness. It is nothing less than an exalted presentation of ones intuition. Like surrealist images, intuition always appears spontaneously.

Since the unconscious tends to speak in metaphors, it is these metaphors which confront us most proficiently with metaphysical subjects. This is so because with all other types of intuition there is a greater tendency to cater to what is immediately rational. Surrealism, in its heightened form, is a means of explicating into physiological consciousness what would otherwise appear as disorder.

The contents of the unconscious can be positive or negative. For this reason there are both positive and negative expressions of surrealism. It is a benefit that through surrealism we can see stark depictions of everyday objects presented indiscriminately in whatever contexts yield themselves. If it is more disturbing to see a phone on a plate than it is to see a moon on a plate, there is a reason. In ancient times, prior to materialistic technology and industry, there were not as many disturbing collages of subject matter latent.

With the rise of the surrealist movement in Europe, the subject matter of dreams was made photo-realistically visible. This was truly, moreso than the psychology or anything else of the times, the means by which all of the repressed components of the European psyche began to resurface.

When we compare nonindustrial societies with the more pedantic societies of historical Europe we should sincerely consider the responsibility we as humans have for the maintenance of our psyches, including the unconscious aspects. The degree to which we have lost touch with the order of nature was made visible, in unexaggerated terms, with the original surrealist movement in Europe. All of the contents therein that disorient us reflect aspects of each of us that we are responsible for. The degree to which we are unfamiliar with these themes is the degree to which we are unfamiliar with ourselves. These images challenge our ideas of the ground that we think we stand on.

Of all existent forms of surrealism the most refined and triumphant is that which celebrates life. This is in contrast to forms which are either against life or which complain about that which is against life. Differentiations between the three forms mentioned are necessary. More upbeat expressions of metaphors lend themselves to a greater and more progressive degree of differentiation. All vital notions are impeded by the other two forms of surrealist expression. It is for this reason that great works of art and science are normally accomplished, in a sense, without effort. Such accomplishments cannot be forced. They take place beyond the realm of conscious obstructions. They happen preternaturally without restrictions, on an ever-mysterious tide of light. The basis of their beauty is that they are implicitly positive examples of spontaneous revelation. In other words, they are reflections of a clean unconscious. From the explication of such constructs, what emerges are not only accurate perspectives, but differentiations that do not involve expressions of those negative qualities which one is dissecting. If one plays a piece of music on a guitar they do not play the wrong notes to show that those notes are wrong. The same applies in all mediums of art and science. One can be perfectly conscious of what is correct or incorrect and can express that consciousness in their work without actually portraying that which they criticize.

In turn, the broadest form of this positive expression could be called abstract expressionist surrealism. It is likened to jazz, because they both, in principle, embrace all modes of positive expression. We are all already inside the surrealist maze. We must face this fact. We must go further into the density to emerge as identities.

This type of surrealism, the literary form of which will be the main focus of this section, is not slippery. It is designed to convey clarity, not obscurity. Its purpose is to orient its audience with the realities of their own unconscious mind, not to disorient them.

Here is a poem by the former Poet Laureate of Mexico, Octavio Paz:

BROTHERHOOD
Homage to Claudius Ptolemy

I am a man: little do I last
and the night is enormous.
But I look up:
the stars write.
Unknowing I understand:
I too am written,
and at this very moment
someone spells me out.

In this poem we have what can seem to be a number of contradictions, which are not explained within the poem. These appearances arise because the poem is metaphysical. How can he "understand" if he is "unknowing"? He lasts "little," yet he is "written" into the eternal picture. In terms of surrealism, we have stars that write, a man who is written and a night that is enormous. All of this is embedded in the supernal philosophy. The only way to clarify any of it is through the supernal philosophy. At the same time, there is another dilemma latent among supernal philosophers, that of becoming so caught up in explanations of details that one forgets the details themselves. More precisely, while focusing on the explanations of one detail the writer forgets the scope of other related details.

We can understand this type of poetry by understanding metaphysical dichotomies. We can become familiar with the work of a poet and see that the poet is metaphysically voluble. From there his most obscure work becomes comprehensible. We can consider certain metaphors and understand that only one or a limited number of dialectical usages can be metaphysically accurate. If we are reading the metaphor in its original language (or, sometimes, even if it is a translation) and it has more than one accurate usage, it is usually intentional. These are "round meanings." They normally exalt each other, as they would in any other type of poetry.

Paz wrote that a poem "does not mean, but engenders meaning, it is language in its purest form." Paz's work is like raw magma from the supernal volcano. Everything of his that has been published is pristine. In his work we see an effort to communicate on a purely functional level. Subsequently, while his command of vocabulary is superb, he frequently repeats words. Archetypal metaphors, such as *sun, moon, water, fire, earth* and *wind* are often used several times in a single poem. They function perfectly as means of communicating the supernal philosophy. These words can have various meanings even within a single poem.

Other poets, including myself, prefer to avoid repeating the same words. I compare this type of poetry to a sculpted version of magma from the same supernal volcano. With this type of poetry the process sometimes consists of arriving at a means of communication, then finding a way to make that communication less repetitive. If one finishes a stanza in which the word *sun* is used and in the next stanza finds that *sun* also communicates that message, he might find a way to incorporate an equally valuable statement that necessitates a different word, maybe one that provides the most contrast with the word *sun*. By contrast, I mean phonetically, visually and in terms of general meaning. Maybe, since sun is a fairly obvious metaphor, the poet will use a more unusual word, like *terragon*. There are many ways of providing literary contrast. Generally, to do so, the poet considers all of the possible contexts within the poem that apply to the particular part. This can also be taken to the level of the poet's entire body of work, or to the level of all of the poetry known, by the poet, to exist.

The language of dreams in undiluted by literal language. It is a direct and ontologically based language because it yields unbiased messages about unconscious realities. Suppose that, at any given moment, a person is innocent and yet vulnerable to corrupt influences. We should not pronounce those latent corrupt influences. We should, instead, exalt the innocence of that person. A phenomenologically unsurpassed way to do this is to make visible the encouraging messages of that individual's unconscious. This is not possible without surrealism because surrealism is the physiologically conscious expression of the same language which dreams consist of. We cannot convey innocence through surrealism unless there is an originally unconscious innocence to express. So, surrealism is a particularly honest form of expression. Here is an excerpt from a poem by Bernardo de Balbuena, a Mexican poet born in 1561 or 1562. The poem is titled *Immortal Springtime and its Tokens*. It is seven pages:

The limpid waters shimmering far and wide,
troubled like to broken looking-glass,
dazzle the sight with trembling radiance,

and, impearled with blanching foam, reveal,
deep in their vitreous transparencies,
lovely naiads wrought with ivory.

They frolick, gambol, and with joyous starts
wanton on the yielding crystal sheen
in countless figures, miens and attitudes.

One from the mantling wave strikes plumes of spray,
another glides along with sidelong stroke,
others course to and fro, or twist, or roll.

One, whose fairness is unparagoned,
with garlands of alternate gold and flowers
wreaths and embellishes her vaunted grace.

This loveliness, these beauties unconfined,
here dwell and take their pleasure all year long,
exempt from fear and discord and alarums,

in a royal plaisaunce which, in very truth,
exceeds in beauty Cyprus and in balm
of clime and excellence of site the world.

In this excerpt we find a use of vernacular comparable to that of Shakespeare. But there are other elements that we do not find in Shakespeare's work. In the first four stanzas of this excerpt there are seven brilliant, ectopic references to the water. There are three references to precious stones, one to ivory, one to flowers and others to other hyperbolic objects. De Balbuena attains a surreal tone through the use of hyperboles. He also combines these hyperboles in an expressionistic manner. This is a way of augmenting the sounds and images. The colors are exceptionally bright, much like the work of the well-known modern Mexican muralists, Diego Rivera, Jose Clemente Orozco and David Alfaro Sequieros. We can see that this is a refined poem. It is more expressionistic than most Shakespearean poetry, but metrically and in every other sense it is as mature as the Work of Byron, Keats or Shelly. It has a polyrhythmic affect. In fact, there seems to be an intended interplay between different stratas of the rhythm, both visual and phonetic. Perhaps the only criticism that can be made of this poem, in comparison to most Shakespearian poetry, is that it is too busy. People said the same thing about Mozart when he first introduced some of his more elaborate compositions. In any case, the work of De Balbuena, like that of other surrealist poets, reflects an ability to maintain harmony between numerous simultaneous levels of rhythm.

In the previous chapters I have touched on the fact that, in reference to chakra development, we must look not only to epitomic expressions but also to signs of influences between chakras. Both in terms of linguistic statements and in terms of the use of language itself.

We have, as the essential source of accurate thought, the local of all orderly and thus intrinsically syllogistic reasoning, the fifth chakra. Syllogistic reasoning is possible, to an extent, at the third and fourth chakras, but its complete potential is at the fifth. The third is limited to empiricism. The fourth is between empiricism and metaphysics. The fifth transcends and includes both.

Attunement to the fifth chakra—consciousness that is at least fourth chakra but is influenced by the fifth—yields invariable indications, including a recognition of the possibility of worldcentric solutions, a use of spiritual hyperboles combined with a sense of ontological responsibility and a regard for the triumph of order and consciousness over polarities, among others.

Signs of the influence of fifth chakra consciousness (mandalic attunement) are the same regardless of the expression in which they are found. The difficult part is finding them. This section is, in part, a study of means of detecting mandalic attunement in literature. Wilber defines "complete metaphysics" the same way that Hegel, Schelling and others have. He says that it must involve the components of "sensory, symbolic and spirit." As I have said, this is a singular point.

Psychology being the most inclusive of all sciences and sensory, symbolic and spirit being necessary to any adequate study of the psyche. But where there has been historically very little attunement to these vital areas of psychological study, in order to assess metaphysical attunement on a type of historical and current bell curve, we must consider metaphysics in all of its pertinent literary aspects. This is not to underscore the importance of Wilber's statements about "complete metaphysics" nor the fact that he has been probably the greatest representative of these and related vital factors of transpersonal psychology and integrative philosophy of the twentieth century. What I am saying is that in our attempt to come to terms with the metaphysical dichotomies that Wilber describes, it is valuable and ultimately necessary to reveal when and where, in the broad historical picture, identical and/or similar forms of consciousness have been indicated. In this section my study of this subject will be (essentially) limited to its literary aspects.

Poetry is the most inclusive area of literature in which to look for signs of mandalic attunement, for reasons that I have partly explained. At the fifth chakra we have a clear picture of the inherent dialogical order of the universe. There is no doubt that divine reason is inherent in nature. If there were we would not be able to speculate about its meanings syllogistically or geometrically. This is to say that we would be limited to empiricism, to a neglect of subjects such as karmic order, how the balance of polarities can be contiguous with ontological progress, and so forth. Fifth chakra attunement means expressing (consciously or otherwise) a sense or awareness of principles which are the results of the recognition of a static, ontological point on which dynamic, epistemological theories can be syllogistically or geometrically based. The person expressing these principles is not necessarily aware of the ontological mechanism of fifth chakra consciousness, but they are attuned to it enough on an unconscious level to express some of the principles that it embodies.

There are many ways to detect expressions of mandalic consciousness. In the supernal philosophy oneness coincides with plurality. In pseudo-supernal philosophy it is common for people to disregard plurality and ones responsibility for metaphysical progress in favor of a pre-ontological version of oneness. This is generally the result of an inability to coordinate statements about oneness and plurality simultaneously. In Wilber's words, "'Since all is one,' said Charlie Manson, 'nothing is wrong.'" Far more people, throughout history and in every respective geography, have arrived at this misunderstanding than have actually understood any syllogistic explanation of the supernal philosophy. So, in distinguishing Mandalically attuned literature from other literature, we must single out verifications of this basis of metaphysical logic.

Just as in the Bible the most well known books are Genesis, the first; and Revelations, the last, we can to look to the beginnings and ends of books for their underlying messages. We can look to the more dramatic scenes in a book, or to events surrounding central characters. Or we can observe what statements are repeated the most. If we are studying poetry, we can look at titles, which sometimes, directly or otherwise, state central themes. In many cases we can look to a writer's entire body of work to see what reflection it bears on a particular opus of theirs.

Surrealism, as I have said, tends to coincide with metaphysics, because it is precisely mandalic consciousness which makes fluent uses of surrealist language possible. Anyone can come up with surrealist images, but to understand them fluently requires a sufficient degree of fifth chakra attunement. Not only is surrealism potentially mandalic, but it does not discriminate between empiricism and metaphysics. Surrealism simply presents the raw contents of the unconscious.

As I have said, its most expansive form is found in cases of immediate innocence. Only the innocent unconscious lends itself to the full potential of surrealism. In this sense surrealism is a means of avoiding repression. Most nonindustrial societies had culturally surrealist expressions and practices, which included abstract surrealism. This was, on their parts, no doubt, for generally effectually therapeutic purposes.

Just as Senghor and Cesaire were surrealist poets, so were many other members of the Negritude movement from various geographies, including the West Indies, Africa and the Indian Ocean. Some prominent surrealist Negritude poets are Leon Laleau, Leon Damas, David Diop and Elolongue Epanya Yondo.

In the United States, in the 1940s, shortly after the beginning of the surrealist movement, a new literary genre emerged. They called themselves the "Beats," and they were unlike anything the "western world" had seen. They were influenced by jazz and Eastern mysticism. The father of this movement was Jack Kerouac. His second novel, *On the Road*, has been called "the Beat Bible." It was published in 1957.

There was a lot of confusion regarding the Beat movement from the beginning. Most of this confusion remains today. The four main figures of this movement, all writers, were Allen Ginsberg, an overt pedophile and exploitationist; William Burroughs, a sadistic heroin addict; Neal Cassidy, a womanizer and hoodlum in general; and Kerouac, who wasn't really like any of the others.

Neal Cassidy was the hero of some of Kerouac's novels, including *On the Road*. I think that, when noting this, it is important to consider cultural context. The story in *On the Road* took place before Rosa Parks. Kerouac's writing after his first novel, *The Town and the City*, which was influenced by Thomas Wolfe, was influenced essentially by jazz, rather than by other writers, with the exception of Neal Cassidy. The only book Cassidy ever wrote was *The First Third: A Partial Autobiography*. *The First Third* exemplifies the literature that inspired Kerouac's work. It was vigorous and full of analyses of unobvious subjects. It tended to be structured in such a way that frenetic patterns of hyphens and parenthesis pervaded long sentences. Like Kerouac's work, it conveyed the same musicality as jazz. Also it was raw, not flowery or political. Its appeal lied more in what he said than the way he said it. It was direct, and it accelerated through that directness. It was this rawness, vigorous analytical quality and reliance on rhythmic momentum and straight subject matter that appealed to Kerouac. After *The Town and the City* Cassidy was basically Kerouac's only literary influence. Cassidy was also the one who introduced the other beats to Eastern mysticism.

Nevertheless, he was a hoodlum, and Kerouac, in his early years, celebrated the fact that Cassidy once escaped from San Quinton Prison and that he once stole five-hundred cars in one year.

The press and numerous scholars, as third chakra consciousness would have it, from the beginning, confused Kerouac with Cassidy and the other notorious figures of the Beat movement. From the beginning Kerouac told the press that he was not like the other Beats, that he was able to write as well as he did only because he lived "a kind of monastic life." In his later years his disposition was the same. He told people that he was never into the "Dionysus" archetype, that he had always preached "piety."

Kerouac was an alcoholic throughout his adult life. He dabbled in hard drugs and was known to take benzadrine inhalers to "help" him write. The two novels that I know of that he wrote under the influence of benzadrine were *On the Road*, which he finished in either two weeks or three weeks, depending on the account; and *The Subterranians*, which he wrote in two nights. Kerouac was notably promiscuous in his younger years, but otherwise respectful to women. He was not really violent, he never beat anyone up or went to jail. Even his writings about the most juvenile adventures depict him as essentially quiet and considerate about ethics. Kerouac's version of a sentence depicting an irresponsible attitude is exemplified in *On the Road* when he and Cassidy steal a few items from a gas station and he writes, "Crooks don't know."

There is a subtle brilliance in Kerouac's adolescent admiration for Cassidy's recklessness. The things that Cassidy did incessantly were, for the most part, things that Kerouac would never do. Ultimately the air of all of these adventures is one of a naïve poet being led by an intelligent yet irresponsible young man who happens to be the only person who really accepts Kerouac and can provide mental stimulation, enjoys jazz as much and so on.

Kerouac's message was not one of irresponsibility. Ultimately he was critical of irresponsibility, regardless of its source. Practically every other beat was a hoodlum. But Kerouac was a compassionate, despite his alcoholism, person. Unlike the works of Ginsberg, Burroughs, Cassidy and others, Kerouac's most pronounced tone was one of responsibility. This can be seen, for example, in the fronts and backs of most of his books. The last "chorus" in *Mexico City Blues* begins with the sentence, "The sound in your mind is the first sound that you could sing if you were singing at a cash register with nothing on yr mind" and ends with the sentences, "Stop the murder and the suicide. All's well. I am the guard." At the end of *On the Road* he writes, "In Iowa I know by now the children must be crying in the land where they let the children cry." This is to say that we should not let the children cry. The works of other prominent beats are riddled with prerational statements. Ginsberg's poems, such as *On Burroughs' Work*, *Metaphysics* and *The Terms in Which I Think of Reality* and Burroughs' work, such as *Nova Express*, which he said stated his message the clearest, are all quasi-rational, at best.

Kerouac's work, however, is full of brilliant statements about the supernal philosophy. He wrote a thousand-page sutra. It is Kerouac who introduced jazz and Eastern philosophy into white culture. He was always accountable for his relatively benevolent mistakes, and should be considered the original integrative philosopher. There was a significant interest in Eastern mysticism among the surrealists and, as I mentioned in chapter one, a particular interest in indigenous cultures and jazz, but none of these influences were nearly as pronounced in the work of the surrealists as they were in that of the Beats. All of these innovations were on a parallel, for Kerouac, with disparate other revolutionary qualities. Ginsberg, for example, admired the Shakespearian poet Ezra Pound, whom Kerouac thought was "pretentious." We're talking about an extremely innovative personality in general.

Ironically, I should perhaps add that Wilber has commended the movie *Trainspotting*, which was based on the novel by Irvine Welsh, the king of the "Scottish beats".

In *Up From Eden* Wilber groups the entire beat movement together under the title of the "Dharma Bums," (Wilber's quotations.) one of Kerouac's novels. In obscure detail he says that they were all "pre-egoic," "narcissistic" and full of "marxist dogma." In a profound sense, he's right. But none of those descriptions fit Kerouac, by any means. In addition, there is nothing mutually exclusive about the terms "dharma" and "bums." One does not need to be unethical to be homeless.

My central observation, however, of Wilber's take on the "Dharma Bums" is that he does not express an appreciation of the exaltation of jazz, or of the fact that it coincided with a new cultural interest in Eastern philosophy, as superficial as the interpretations of both dominantly were.

Wilber misinterpreted Kerouac's work similarly to the way he misinterpreted Jung's work, except that with Kerouac's work he did it on two mutually distinct levels. First he underestimated Kerouac's skill as a metaphysical philosopher. Then, because he was not aware that jazz was the fifth chakra form of music, he did not understand why the original fusion of elements of black culture into white culture coincided with the popularity of Kerouac's work.

Here is a song by Sun Ra:

Rise lightly from the earth
And try your wings
Try them now
While I make the darkness invisible
The visibility of day
Is the invisibility of night
The invisibility of day
Is the visibility of night
So rise lightly from the earth
And try your wings
Try them now
While the darkness is invisible

These lyrics are phenomenological. We cannot tell by studying them alone whether or not Sun Ra understood phenomenology, but the lyrics in themselves suggest that he might have. If we study other writings of his—lyrics, poems or his *Book of Intergalactic Wisdom*—or if we study interviews with him, we can see that he was, in fact, a remarkable metaphysical philosopher. The same is true for a broad number of jazz musicians and surrealist and Negritude writers.

Edward Braithwaite is a poet from the West Indies. His most well known book is *To Sir With Love*, which was made into a movie that starred Sidney Poitier. Here is an excerpt from his poem *Korabra*:

So for my hacked
face, hollowed eyes,
undrumming heart,

make me a black
mask that dreams
silence,

reflects no light,
smiles no pretense,
hears not my brother's

language.
Let me without
my mother's

blood, my father's
holy kra, traverse
paths where yet

the new dead
cannot know that
time was evil,

but where dew's
ears prepare
for my coming.

Any adequately observant phenomenologist can notice a profound use of dialectical images: mother and father, blood and kra, language and pretense. Also, in a confident voice Braithwaite makes statements such as, "Where the new dead cannot know that time was evil." The concept of time being evil in its finite sense is, in itself, phenomenological. But when he adds to it that the "new dead" cannot know that it was evil, this can only convey an understanding (conscious or otherwise) that the dead, if not freed from cause and effect, are, like any other holonic beings, capable of not understanding that finite time itself is what we all must eventually transcend.

Braithwaite does not explain any of this explicitly. He simply says, "the new dead," rather than saying formally that he means the non-metaphysically conscious dead. He says "time," rather than explaining formally that he means holonic or finite time. He explains all of this, but he does it in functional, poetic language. At the end of the passage he is speaking about transcending non-metaphysically conscious, disembodied beings in favor of metaphysical consciousness.

This type of poetry is subtle, sometimes intentionally understated. The reason for this is usually that these poets have such powerful commands of metaphysics that to explicate in conventional terms every profound metaphysical revelation that occurred to them in the course of writing a poem would only slow down the progress of the greater metaphysical scope available to them. By bypassing academic explications of their thought processes they are able to better reflect their true psychological states. This allows them to use various metaphysical means of expressing a broader amount of metaphysical concepts. These means and concepts are all compatible with Wilber's ladder paradigm, but most of them are beyond Wilber's vocabulary.

Poets of the black diaspora, from Saro-Wiwa and Soyinka to the Negritude poets to the poets of the Harlem Renaissance to modern poets like Jordan and Lorde, have very consistently expressed prodigious metaphysical attunement.

Popular hip-hop music today, collectively, is a case study in how a mass mockery of a genocide can emerge in response to mass narcissism. Hip-hop artists like Nas, et al. produce atrocious lyrics. It is slander to compare them to blues musicians like Mississippi John Hurt, William Hudson "Leadbelly" Ledbetter, Muddy Waters, Robert Johnson, etc.

Likewise, the lyrics of some of the better popular Masters of Ceremony (M.C.s) today—i.e., KRS-One, Black Thought, etc.—do not compare to the poetry of, say, Harlem Renaissance poets like Langston Hughes, Claude McKay, Anne Spencer, et al.

There are all sorts of malignant things sprouting up from hip-hop. For example, there is evidently a global virtual subculture that, in a bizarre and morbid display of pseudo-progressiveness, insists that Tupac Shakur's *Codes of the Thug Life*—a one-and-a-half page document effactually calling for "ethical" turf warfare—is the instruction manual for the contemporary equivalent of the Black Panther Party for Self-Defense (BPP) while not making any effort to learn what living former prominent members of the BPP—i.e., Bobby Seale and Davis— have to say about the matter and, further, being—generally covertly—hostile toward anyone who tries to tell them.

Incidentally, for those who ultimately do not like the genocide in the U.S.—
which is for the most part black on black, though systemically essentially white
on black—Davis says this of hip-hop culture, "Where is the door—or even the
window—opening onto a conception of political practice?"

*It is clear that Tupac never had a genuine allegiance to the spirit of the Panthers
and that his mom, Afeni Shakur—who, as many people know, is a former member of the Panthers—does not either* (Dyson, 2003; Guy, 2004).

Hip-hop—a genre that embodies music, dance (breakdancing) and visual art
(graffiti)—began in the Bronx, New York in the early seventies as a means to
stand against gang violence. In the early days of hip-hop—until about the mid
1980s—artists like Grandmaster Flash, Kurtis Blow, Grandmaster Melle Mel,
Kool Moe Dee, Whodini and Roxanne Shante consistently expressed positive
messages in their lyrics, were highly inventive musically, etc. (These artists did
also express the realities of ghettos in the U.S. to the public at large. KRS-One
cites Grandmaster Melle Mel's song *The Message* in regard to this fact. But the
non-lumpen proletariat public at large, as we will see, basically did much worse
than turn a deaf ear.) This was before people shot at each other in inner-cities
throughout the country anywhere near as much as they do today. This was also
up until around the time that COINTELPRO, as the Senate Select Committee
put it (Jackson, 1996), "engaged in lawless tactics against the Black Panther
Party." (The BPP was shut down in the early to mid 1980s.)

Gangsta rap originated in California—Compton, Oakland, etc.—in the late
eighties.

Classic examples of early gangsta rap albums include N.W.A.'s *Straight Outta
Compton* and Ice T's *Power*.

Here I will give the reader some idea of the political climate in the U.S. today.

Only about 12.5% of the total U.S. population is black (Let us not try to revert
to one-drop rule loop-holes. We know what the gene pool is like in Watts, what
it's like in Beverly Hills and that it is basically like this throughout the country.); however, approximately one third of the total U.S. population below the
poverty level is black. According to West and Manning Marable one in every
two black children in the U.S. lives in poverty. Blacks commit about 12% of the
total drug crimes in the U.S. and do about 70% of the drug sentences. Around
80% of the people on death row are black men, and blacks constitute 42% of the
people in prison in the U.S. There are well over 180,000 more black than white
people in state and federal prisons in the country.

As Davis puts it, black Americans have gone "from the prison of slavery to the slavery of prison". When they are arrested for crimes they did not commit they are at least very commonly, if not typically, coerced by public defenders to perjure themselves, often in attempts to get their cases off the docket as soon as possible. When they are convicted, if they get out of jail or prison they no longer have various basic human rights that other members of the populace normally have. And it is much, much worse; one could of course go on indefinitely about these and directly related subjects.

White people throughout the U.S. seem to be generally sort of covertly ostensibly unable to register the type of census data mentioned. They quote King, then talk about how many poor white farmers there are; there is considerable talk among them about the *military industrial complex* but scarcely any sensible discussion among them about the *prison industrial complex* (the local flip-side of the military industrial complex). Apparently the popular white liberal slogan, "Think globally, act locally." Does not apply to the holocausts and low intensity warfare that are happening in lumpen proletariat areas throughout the country. There is all of the racial and cultural profiling, the Rockefeller drug laws, *et al.*

Regardless of the reasons, contemporary popular rap, as a whole—despite the *Self-Destruction* single, an anti-gang song orchestrated by KRS-One in 1989 that featured numerous recording artists, including Public Enemy, Kool Moe Dee, Digital Underground, M.C. Lyte, Just Ice and, of course, KRS-One and Boogie Down Productions and despite progressive hip-hop artists like Public Enemy, Lauryn Hill, Digable Planets (Butterfly from Digable Planets raps, "Check out some Frantz, some Sartre, Camus."), Arrested Development, etc.—has become regressive/violently dissociative.

Basically, the world has witnessed in rap a genre of "poetry" (Whether or not the word *poetry* can be used in this context depends on whether or not we can call the average popular rap lyrics today poetry.) that began as a brilliant, original and integrative art form, resembling haiku in its simplicity, but clearly being an extension of jazz (Ngoma, the traditional African call-and-response pattern, is found throughout the history of rap, etc.), become regressive in a span of about twenty years.

The vocabulary, in terms of verbal musicality, expressed in the works of, say, Beat poets like Kerouac, Ginsberg or Lawrence Ferlinghetti is vastly beyond that of the average popular rapper today. Here I am referring to the various strains and swing rhythms, the understanding of indigenous musicality, etc. expressed in the works of the major Beat poets of Kerouac's generation. (In my view, supposed Beat poetry today at slam poetry readings, etc. is generally violently anti-progressive.)

The popular hip-hop group Wu-Tang Clan, for example, has lyrics that make them sound, literally, like fundamentalist Muslim pimps—in their song *Sunshower*, etc.

Clearly, what is happening in regard to the hip-hop music industry, more or less, is that the public is effectually demanding genocide, the record industry, being a money-making industry, is producing it, and it is being sold. (Young non-lumpen proletariats in the U.S. never got anywhere near as into pre-gangsta rap hip-hop as they have been into gangsta rap for more than the past decade, and so on.)

Hip-hop music as it exists today is making it infinitely more difficult for actual progressive people to survive than it would otherwise be. The more or less extremely covert pseudo-progressiveness that its proponents collectively express is actually reminiscent of white feminism.

Major figures associated with the Rastafarian religion—i.e., Leonard P. Howell, H.I.M. Haile Selassie, Marcus Garvey, Robert Nesta Marley, Bunny Wailer, etc.—are evidently at the fifth chakra.

There is much that could be elaborated upon, from the Hegelianism of Walt Whitman (Whitman was racist toward Mexicans (ironically enough, since there are at least a good number of prominent Mexican poets, historical and modern, whom Whitman definitely has nothing on.); but he appears to have not been racist against blacks—i.e., in *I Sing the Body Electric*.) to Cesar Vallejo's word *trilce*, which some scholars interpret as being a metaphysical number which translates as 00.1 or similar. (The formula is: 0 (self as subjective, thanatos, thesis) + 0 (other as subjective, thanatos, antithesis) = 1 (synthesis). Or: 0 (self as subjective, thanatos, thesis) + 0 (self as relatively objective, thanatos, antithesis) = 1 (synthesis). Etc.)

Poetry is a powerful means of individuation; and it is a literary means that oppressed people are often more or less limited to. Thereby it should be no surprise that all of this metaphysical consciousness has existed/does exist in the literary and oral traditions discussed, evidently very far from the "progressive" mainstream. In fact, the greatest surrealist poets, globally, have generally been at the upper fourth or fifth chakra. (This is something that prominent surrealists have in common with prominent jazz musicians.)

The lack of attunement to what the Negritude, surrealist and Beat poets, poets of the Harlem Renaissance, etc. really stood for in mainstream and, by and large, popular scholarship at large merely illustrates how dissociated industrialized societies are and underscores the urgency with which the human species must again become authentically mindful of the unconscious—which, at the fifth chakra, corresponds to the ontology. (Fifth chakra consciousness of the fact that there is something outside of ones subjectivity more or less is consciousness of the ontology.)

Poets like Senghor, Paz, Lima, Jordan, Lorde, *et al.* also write exquisite academia. Maybe in the not too distant future the scholars who run the academic show will consistently express this type of hemispheric balance, attunement to the unconscious and integrative approach toward the *other*.

Conclusion

Homo sapiens sapiens originated in Africa at least 100,000 years B.C. There is no evidence that the species' sense of temporality has become any greater—which would strongly suggest that it has become more conscious. On the contrary, judging from the difference between the earliest written metaphysics—i.e., in Kemet and India—and the metaphysical thought and practices of indigenous priests and the preposterous ideologies that pass for metaphysics among our "greatest minds" today and other abundant and eclectic evidence (historical, geological, anthropological, genealogical, archeological, neurological, osteological, paleoclimatological, *et al.*), the human species' sense of temporality has decreased profoundly, Europe and the Near East have been regressing for hundreds of years, etc.

Collective dissociations began in Europe, the Near East and, to a much lesser degree, China cir. 1000 to 500 B.C. The collective dissociation in Europe (I generally use the term *European dissociation*—which was actually coined by Wilber—to refer to the dissociation in Europe and the one in the Near East.) became a collective regression around 1450 A.D. The collective dissociation in the Near East became a collective regression around the same time, roughly. (I have to concede that I lack the historical knowledge of the Near East necessary to give a very precise estimation of when the collective regression began there. (A lot of historical knowledge relevant to the subject is shrouded—i.e., regarding the origin of infibulation.) All of Mediterranean Africa was conquered by Arabic Muslims in the seventh century, the century Islam was founded, *et al.* Yet, otherwise progressive scholars—Cesaire, etc.—have and do often overlook(ed) how violently dissociative of the *other* Near Easterners—collectively—have been historically and are today.) However, the collective dissociation in China did not become a collective regression until after the turn of the twentieth century, after Asian countries started to become industrialized.

Overwhelming eclectic evidence suggests that most traditional African societies prior to colonial influence were, as apparently more or less every prominent member of the ABP says, consubstantiative.

Most likely the natural mode of human societies has been consubstantiative since not long after the emergence of verbal language, perhaps sometime around 50,000 B.C.

In terms of chakra theory—based on complete metaphysics, et al. and drawing from the views of the chakra system put forth in works by Nelson, Wilber, Bynum, Laing, Jung, Akbar, Feuerstein, etc., and from those expressed in ancient Kemetic and Hindu texts, and so on—it is safe to say that any genuinely consubstantiative society would have to be at at least the upper third or lower fourth chakra.

I agree with Nelson's statement (1994) that most industrialized people will never evolve beyond the third chakra. For all of the libraries and material technology *our supposed authorities on psychology and philosophy, while usually claiming to have the highest regard for the works of Socrates, etc. are, by and large, light years from actually grasping things like Aristotle's concept of "first science" or Plotinus' concept of the "virtue of Wisdom" versus the "natural virtues."* And they are generally—with exceptions that are virtually too rare to mention—terrified of looking judicially at the connotations of ancient Kemetic, Hindu and historical and existent traditional African and other indigenous metaphysics.

It is vital that much more interviews with what Oruka calls "sage philosophers" and indigenous women who know their traditions be conducted. But, at least in the former case, they must be conducted by philosophers who are skilled with metaphysics.

Right now there is much that we can tell about the traditional metaphysics of the Akan, Yoruba, Shona, Igbo, et al., but, at once, there are huge discrepancies between Gyekye and Wiredu's accounts of traditional Akan metaphysics, and so on.

It is as Mbembe (2001) writes, "… the problem is not that Western thought posits the *self* (self-identity) as *other than the other*. Nor does everything come down to a simple opposition between truth and error, or to a confrontation between reason and that form of unreason called fable or even madness. In fact, here is a principle of language and classificatory systems in which to *differ* from something or somebody is not simply *not to be like* (in the sense of being non-identical or being other); it is also *not to be at all* (non-being)."

Monotheism, verbal language, syllogistic reasoning (including mathematics), *the supernal philosophy* (in both its ontological and pre-ontological expressions), *civilization, et al. originated in black Africa*—probably tens of thousands of years B.C. Inventions generally attributed to Europeans, from geometry and agriculture to phonograms and written history, also originated in black Africa (Bynum, 1999, *et al.*).

At the same time black people are by far the most violently oppressed and stigmatized ethnic group the world over.

I have given a cohesive, if laconic, overview of the role of the indigenous African psyche in the evolution of human consciousness. And in doing this I have integrated into my own—ontological—system (which is based on traditional African, ancient Hindu, etc. metaphysics) Jung's spiral paradigm (for all means and purposes), numerous valuable metaphysical ideas put forth by authors like Amo, Fanon, Laing, Akbar, Wilber, Breton, etc., much of the chakra theory of Bynum, Nelson, Wilber, Akbar, etc. (As we have seen, Wilber, for example, despite his Eurocentrism, has introduced metaphysical and other ideas into popular psychology that are vital to cross-cultural and gender psychology, etc.), and so on. But I have also presented support for my assertions based on indigenous people's accounts of their own cultures and histories, with a particular focus on accounts by indigenous priests, elders and women, the anthropology/ sociology of scholars like Horton, Ohadike, Tempels, Jahn, Levi-Strauss, etc., comparative mind-body integration, art history, and so on.

In short, the assertions made in this book are based on an eclectic range of both empirical and metaphysical evidence.

I have addressed subjects ranging from the philosophies of various figures of the black diaspora and other progressive figures and metaphysical and ethnological consciousness in art, music and literature to female genital mutilation in Africa and elsewhere, traditional African "palliative"—as Asante calls them— unifying processes and comparative European and Asian cultural traits.

The reality is that while there were, of course, some feudalistic socio-political systems in traditional Africa there were at once *pronounced* egalitarian elements in societies throughout the continent—i.e., the Khoisan, Sao,!Kung, Akan, Maasai, Yoruba, Mbuti, Tuareg, et al. In fact, even clearly racist scholars—i.e., Margery Perham (Perham and Simmons (Eds.), 1963)—effectually depict traditional African socio-political systems as having very consistently embodied marked egalitarian elements.

I have addressed the problem of pseudo-progressive masses globally who are clearly *and* covertly—if one can imagine—ridiculing ethnological issues at large rather than approaching them in a rational manner.

This is standard "new racism"/neocolonialism. And it is promulgated not only by mainstream in general and, by and large, (genuinely) popular scholars at large but also by those who ardently go in for the "new science"—in which there is, for example, no way to establish a necessity for ethics—while being clearly—though, of course, generally covertly—adverse to hearing what indigenous people say about their own traditional world views, by people who *insist* that Carlos Castaneda is a major authority on Amerindian shamanism, despite the fact that his work, while having received a lot of praise from Deepak Chopra and *The New York Times, has apparently not been endorsed by a single indigenous person, let alone a Yaqui shaman,* by all sorts of "democrats," liberals, "environmentalists," human rights activists, "feminists," people who make the racist presumption that indigenous people were anarchists prior to colonial influence (which includes a lot of young people in the First World, a huge percentage of whom are explicitly anti-democratic.), and so on. This situation has a lot to do with guiding fictions, as stated in chapters two and three. Whether or not we are evolving or even regressing is determined by whether we are integrating the *other* more or dissociating it more, for ultimately the integration of the *other* lapses into the integration of Spirit and, contiguously, genuine conscience. It is arguable that most of the oppression on the planet today is enforced strictly by way of epistemic violence (malignant, phony, Afrophobic, politically-correct knowledge bases and so on). Expressions of the types of pseudo-progressiveness discussed—whether in magazines like *What is Enlightenment?* or *The Sun* or wherever—must be clearly identified, and their proponents' academic cards must be called.

In this book I have extolled, to some pervasive degree, where various factions of the human species were in their paths of spiritual evolution prior to different collective dissociations and regressions. I have done this not in an attempt to turn back the clock but rather *in order to reveal and define what psychological mark we must aim for a translation of in order to evolve again collectively as a species.*

Bibliography

Abraham, W.E. (1962). *The mind of Africa*. London: Weidenfeld and Nicolson

Abdalla, R.H.D. (1982). *Sisters in affliction: Circumcision and infibulation of women in africa*. London: Zed Press

Akbar, N. (1994). *Light from ancient africa*. Tallahassee, FL: Mind Productions & Associates, Inc.

Akbar, N. (1995). *Natural psychology and human transformation*. Tallahassee, FL: Mind Productions & Associates, Inc.

Anglesey, Z. (Ed.). (1999). *Listen up!: Spoken word poetry*. New York: One World

Anozie, S.O. (1982). *Phenomenology in modern african studies*. New York: Conch Magazine Limited

Appiah, K.A. (2003). *Thinking it through: An introduction to contemporary philosophy*. Oxford: Oxford University Press

Asante, M.K. (1987). *The afrocentric idea*. Philadelphia: Temple University Press

Azibo, D.A. (1996). *African psychology in historical perspective & related commentary*. Trenton: AfricaWorld Press, Inc.

Balakian, A. (1947). *Literary origins of surrealism: A new mysticism in french poetry*. NewYork: New York University Press

Balakian, A. (1986). *Surrealism: The road to the absolute*. Chicago: The University of Chicago Press

Basham, A.L. (1963). *The wonder that was india: A study of the history and culture of the indian sub-continent before the coming of the muslims*. New York: Hawthorn Books

Bayly, C.A. (Ed.) (1990). *The raj: India and the british 1600-1947*. London: National Portrait Gallery Publications

Beattie, J. (1960). *Bunyoro: An african kingdom*. New York: Holt, Rinehart and Winston

Beck, L.J. (1965). *The metaphysics of descartes: A study of the meditations.* New York: Oxford University Press

Benedikt, M. (1974). *The poetry of surrealism: An anthology.* Boston: Little, Brown and Company

Berrian, A.H.; Long, R.A. (1967). *Negritude: Essays and studies.* Hampton, VI: Hampton Institute Press, 1967

Berry, J. (1991). *West african folktales.* Evanston, IL: Northwestern University Press

Bettis, J.D. (1969). *Phenomenology of religion: Eight modern descriptions of the essence of religion.* New York: Harper & Row Publishers

Blacker, C. (1999). *The catalpa bow: A study of shamanic practices in japan.* Malta: Interprint Limited

Blakely, T.D.; van Beek, W.E.A. and Thomson, D.L. (Eds.). (1994). *Religion in africa.* Portsmouth: Heinemann

Blofeld, J. (1970). *The tantric mysticism of tibet.* New York: E.P. Dutton & Co., Inc

Boas, F. (1938). *The mind of primitive man.* New York: The Macmillan Company

Bodunrin, P.O. (1981). *The question of African philosophy.* New York: Philosophy

Bohm, D. (1971). *Causality and chance in modern physics.* Philadelphia: University of Pennsylvania Press Philadelphia

Bond, M.H. (Ed.) (1996). *The handbook of chinese psychology.* New York: Oxford University Press

Braithwaite, E. (1973). *The arrivants: A new world trilogy.* London: Oxford University Press

Breton, A. (1977). *Manifestos du surrealism.* Michigan: University of Michigan Press

Brown, L.M. (Ed.). (2004). *African philosophy: New and traditional perspectives.* New York: Oxford University Press

Bucher, H. (1996). *Spirits and power: An analysis of shona cosmology.* Cape Town: Oxford University Press

Burlew, A.K.H.; Banks, W.C.; McAdoo, H.P.; Azibo, D.A. (1992). *African American psychology: Theory, research, and practice.* Newbury Park, CA: SAGE Publications

Bynum, E.B. (1999). *The african unconscious: Roots of ancient mysticism and modern psychology*. New York: Teacher's College Press

Campbell, J. (1969). *The masks of god: Primitive mythology*. New York: The Viking Press

Campbell, J. (1988). *An open life*. Burdett, N.Y: Larson Publications

Canty, J.M. (2000). *Cultural ecopsychology: Issues of displacement and the urban African american community*.

Chang, J. (2005). *Can't stop won't stop: A history of the hip-hop generation*. New York: St. Martin's Press

Clark, R.W. (1971). *Einstein: The life and times*. New York: World Publishing

Coetzee, P.H. and Roux, A.P.J. (1998). *The african philosophy reader*. New York: Routledge

Coole, D. (1993). *Women in political theory: From ancient misogyny to contemporary feminism*. Boulder: Lynn Rienner Publishers, Inc.

Cott, J. (1994). *Isis and osiris: Exploring the goddess myth*. New York: Doubleday

Coulson, D. and Campbell, A. (2001). *African rock art: Paintings and engravings in stone*. New York: Harry N. Abrams, Inc.

Crow, M. (1988). *Woman who has sprouted wings: Poems by contemporary latin american women poets*. Pittsburgh: Latin American Literary Review Press

Da Free John (1980). *Scientific proof of the existence of god will soon be announced by the whitehouse*. New York: Dawn Horse Press

Davidson, B. (1969). *The african genius*. London: Little, Brown and Co.

Davidson, B. (1968,1974). *Africa in history*. New York: Macmillan Publishing Company.

Davidson, B. and the editors of Time-Life Books (1966). *African kingdoms*. New York: Time Inc.

Davis, A.Y. (2003). *Are prisons obsolete?* New York: Seven Stories Press.

Davis, A.Y. (1998). *The angela y. davis reader*. Oxford: Blackwell Publishers Ltd.

Deax, K. (1976). *The behavior of women and men*. Monterey, CA: Brooks/Cole Publishing Company

Deppert, J. (Ed.). (1983). *India and the west: Proceedings of a seminar dedicated to the memory of herman goetz*. New Delhi: Manohar

De Waal, F.B.M. (2001). *Tree of origin: What primate behavior can tell us about human social evolution.* Cambridge and London: Harvard University Press

Du Bois, W.E.B. (1915). *The negro.* New York: Henry Holt and Company

Dunbar, R. and Barrett, L. (2000). *Cousins: Our primate relatives.* London: BBC Worldwide Ltd

Dyson, Michael Eric. (2003). *Holler if you hear me: Searching for tupac shakur.* New York: Basic Civitas Books

Ebrey, P.B. (1996). *The cambridge history of china.* Cambridge, MA: Cambridge University Press

Ebrey, P.B. (1993). *The inner quarters: Marriage and the lives of chinese women in the sung period.* Berkeley: University of California Press

Eccles, J.C. (1991). *Evolution of the brain: Creation of the self.* New York: Routledge

Einstein, A. (1954). *Ideas and opinions.* New York: Crown Publishers, Inc.

Eller, C. (2000). *The myth of matriarchal prehistory: Why an invented past won't give women a future.* Boston: Beacon Press

Erikson, E.H. (1973). *In search of common ground: Conversations with erik h. erikson and huey p. newton.* New York: W.W. Norton & Company, Inc.

Fanon, F. (1968). *The wretched of the earth.* New York: Grove Press, Inc.

Farber, M. (1967). *Phenomenology and existence: Toward a philosophy within nature.* New York: Harper Torchbooks

Faulkner, R.O. (1969). *The ancient egyptian pyramid texts.* London: Oxford University Press

Feuerstein, G. (1990). *Encyclopedic dictionary of yoga.* New York: Paragon House

Feuerstein, G. (1987). *Structures of consciousness: The genius of jean gebser.* Lower Lake, CA: Integral Publishing

Ford, C.W. (1999). *The hero with an african face: Mythic wisdom of traditional africa.* New York: Bantum Books

Fortes, M. (1983). *Oedipus and job in west african religion.* New York: Cambridge University Press

Freud, S. (1962). *The ego and the id.* New York: W.W. Norton & Company, Inc.

Gadamer, H. (1994). *Heidegger's ways.* Albany, N.Y.: State University of New York Press

Gates, Jr., H.L.; West, C. (1996). *The future of the race.* New York: Vintage
Books

Gilbert, E. and Reynolds, J. (2004). *Africa in world history: From prehistory to
present.* Upper Saddle River, N.J.: Pearson/Prentice Hall

Gilligan, C. *The birth of pleasure.* (2002). New York: Alfred A. Knopf

Goldman, L.R. and Ballard, C. (1998). *Fluid ontologies: Myth, ritual and philosophy in the highlands of papua new guinea.* Westport: Bergin & Garvey

Gordon, L.R.; Sharpley-Whiting, T.D. and White, R.T. (1996). *Fanon: A critical
reader.* Cambridge, MA.: Blackwell Publishers

Gould, S.J. (1977). *Ontogeny and phylogeny.* Cambridge, MA: The Belknap
Press of Harvard University Press

Graves, J.R. (2001). The *emperor's new clothes: Biological theories of race at the
millennium.* New Jersey: Rutgers University Press

Greenberg, J.H. (1967). *Essays in linguistics.* Chicago: The University of Chicago
Press

Griaule, M. (1965). *Conversations with ogotemmeli: An introduction to dogon
religious ideas.* London: Oxford University Press

Gunn, G. (1979). *The interpretation of otherness: Literature, religion, and the
American Imagination.* New York: Oxford University Press

Guy, J. (2004). *Afeni shakur: Evolution of a revolutionary.* New York: Atria
Books

Gyekye, K. (1995) *An essay on African philosophical thought: the akan concep-
tual scheme.* Philadelphia: Temple University Press

Gyekye, K. (1997). *Tradition and modernity: Philosophical reflections and the
African experience.* New York: Oxford University Press

Harley, S. (1995). *The timetables of african american history.* New York: Simon
& Schuster

Haskins, J. (1997). *Power to the people: The rise and fall of the black panther
party.* New York: Simon & Schuster Books for Young Readers

Haskins, J. and Biondi, J. (1995). *From afar to zulu: A dictionary of african cultures.* New York: Walker and Company

Hegel, G.W.F. (1995). *Lectures on the history of philosophy vol. I.* Lincoln:
University of Nebraska Press

Hegel, G.W.F. (1967). *Philosophy of right.* New York: Oxford University Press

Heidegger, M. (1977). *The question concerning technology and other essays*. New York: Harper & Row

Herman, J. (1997). *Trauma and recovery*. New York: Basic Books

Herodotus. (1928). *The history*. London: Longmans

Herskovits, M.J. (1958). *The myth of the negro past*. Boston: Beacon Press

Hilliard, D. and Weise, D. (2002). *The huey p. newton reader*. New York: Seven Stories Press

Houston, L. (1990). *Psychological principles and the black experience*. New York: University Press of America

Huggins, N.I. (1976). *Voices from the harlem renaissance*. New York: Oxford University Press

Imbo, S.O. (1998). *An introduction to african philosophy*. Boulder: Rowman & Littlefield

Jackson, K.(1996). *America is me: 170 fresh questions and answers on black American history*. New York: HarperCollins Publishers

Jahn, J. (1961). *Muntu: The new african culture*. New York: Grove Press, Inc.

Jammer, M. (1999). *Einstein and religion*. New Jersey: Princeton University Press

Jaynes, J. (2000). *The origin of consciousness in the breakdown of the bicameral mind*. New York: Houghton Mifflin Company

Jenkins, A.H. (1995). *Turning corners: The psychology of african americans*. Boston: Allyn and Bacon

Joll, A. (1999). *Lucy's legacy: Sex and intelligence in human evolution*. Cambridge, Massachusetts & London, England: Harvard University Press

Jones, L. and Neal, L. (Eds.) (1968). *Black fire: An anthology of afro-american writing*. New York: William Morrow & Company, Inc.

Jones, R. (1972). *Black psychology*. New York: Harper & Row Publishers

Jordan, J. (1981). *Civil wars*. Boston: Beacon Press

Josselyn, I.M. *Psychosocial development of children*. (1971). New York: Family Service Association of America

Jung, C.G. (1964). *Man and his symbols*. New York: Doubleday & Company Inc.

Jung, C.G. (1989). *Memories, dreams, reflections*. New York: Vintage

Kalsched, D. (1996). *The inner world of trauma: Archetypal defenses of the personal spirit.* New York: Routledge

Katzner, K. (1977). *The languages of the world.* New York: Routledge

Kebede, M. (2004). *Africa's quest for a philosophy of decolonization.* Amsterdam: Rodopi

Keely, J. (2001). *Rap music.* San Diego: Lucent Books, Inc.

Kennedy, E.C. (1974). *Black writers in french.* Philadelphia: Temple University Press

Kennedy, E.C. (1989). *The negritude poets.* New York: Thunder's Mouth Press

Knappert, J. (1989). *Kings, gods and spirits from african mythology.* New York: Schocken Books

Koslow, P. (1999). *African american desk reference.* New York: The Stone Song Press, Inc.

Lacan, J. (1978). The *four fundamental concepts of psycho-analysis.* New York: W.W. Norton & Company, Inc.

Laing, R.D. (1968). *The politics of experience.* New York: Ballantine Books, Inc.

Lavezzoli, P. (2001). *The king of all, sir duke*: Ellington and the artistic revolution.* New York: Continuum

Leach, E. (1970). *Claude levi-strauss.* New York: The Viking Press, Inc.

Levine, P. (1997) *Waking the tiger.* Berkeley: North Atlantic Books

Levi-Strauss, C. (1966). *The savage mind.* Chicago: The University of Chicago Press

Lewis, D.L. (1993). *W.E.B. du bois (1868-1919): Biography of a race.* New York: Henry Holt and Company, LLC

Lincoln, B. (1999). *Theorizing myth: Narrative, ideology, and scholarship.* Chicago: The University of Chicago Press

Lock, G. (1999). *Blutopia: Visions of the future and revisions of the past in the work of sun ra, duke ellington, and anthony braxton.* Durham & London: Duke University Press

Lugira, A.M. (1999). *African religion: World religions.* New York: Facts on File, Inc.

Lukacs, G. (1971). *History and class consciousness: Studies in marxist dialectics.* Great Britain: The Merlin Press Ltd.

Magesa, L. (1997). *African religion: The moral traditions of abundant life*. New York: Orbis Books

Maja-Pearce, A. (Ed.). *The heinemann book of african poetry in English*. (1990). London: Heinemann

Marcus, J. and Tarr, Z. (1989). *Georg lukacs theory, culture, and politics*. New Brunswick: Transaction

Mbembe, A. (2001). *On the postcolony*. Berkeley: University of California Press

Meyerowitz, E.L.R. (1958). *The akan of ghana: Their ancient beliefs*. London: Faber & Faber Limited

Michel, J. (2000). *The black surrealists*. New York: Peter Lang Publishing, Inc.

Middleton, J. (1970). *Black africa: Its people and their cultures today*. London: Macmillion

Miles, J.H.; Davis, J.J.; Ferguson-Roberts, S.E.; Giles, R.G. (2001). *Almanac of African american heritage*. Oakland: Prentice Hall

Moghaddam, F.M.; Taylor, D.M. and Wright, S.C. ((1993). *Social psychology in cross cultural perspective*. New York: W.H. Freeman and Company

Mosley, A.G. (Ed.). (1995). *African philosophy: Selected readings*. Englewood Cliffs, N.J.: Prentice Hall

Myers, L.J. (1993). *Understanding an afrocentric worldview: Introduction to an optimal psychology*. Dubuque: Kendall/Hunt

Nance, J. (1975). *The gentle tasaday: A stone age people in the philippine rain forest*.

New York: Harcourt Brace Jovanovich, Inc.

Nelson, J.E. (1994). *Healing the split: Integrating spirit into our understanding of the Mentally ill*. New York: State University of New York Press

Newkirk, P. (2000). *Within the veil: Black journalists, white media*. New York: New York University

Nwala, T.U. (1985) *Igbo philosophy*. Lagos: Lantern Books

Nwala, T.U. (Ed.). (1990). *Treatise on the art of philosophising soberly and accurately*.

Nsukka: The William Amo Center for African Philosophy

Nobles, W.W. (1986). *African psychology: Toward its reclamation, reascention & Revitalization*. Oakland: Black Family Institute

Obenga, T. (2000). *African philosophy during the period of the pharaohs, 2800-330 b.c.* London: Karnac House

Ohadike, D. (1994) *Anioma: A social history of the western igbo people.* Athens: Ohio University Press

Ojaide, T. and Sallah, T.M. (1999). *The new african poetry: An anthology.* Boulder, CO.: Lynne Rienner Publishers, Inc.

Oppert, G. (1978). *On the original inhabitants of bharatavarsa or india.* New York: Arno Press.

Ornstein, R. (1991). *The evolution of consciousness: On darwin, freud and cranial fire: The origins of the way we think.* New York: Prentice Hall Press

Ornstein, R. (1997). *The right mind: Making sense of the hemispheres.* New York: Harcourt Brace and Company

Oyewumi, O. (Ed.). (2003). *African women and feminism: Reflecting on the politics of sisterhood.* Asmara: Africa World Press

Palmer, R.E. (Ed.). (1969). *Hermeneutics.* Evanston: Northwestern University Press

Parham, T.A.; White, J.L.; Ajamu, A. (1999). *The psychology of blacks: An African centered perspective.* Upper Saddle River, N.J.: Prentice Hall

Parrinder, G. (1973). *African mythology.* London: The Hamlyn Publishing Group Ltd

Parrinder, G. (1951). *West african psychology.* London: Lutterworth Press

Paz, O. *Conjunctions and disjunctions.* (1982). New York: Little, Brown and Company

Paz, O. *The bow and the lyre.* (1973). Austin: University of Texas Press

Perham, M. and Simmons, J. (Eds.). (1963). *African discovery: An anthology of exploration.* London: Faber and Faber

Piaget, J. (1965). *The moral judgement of the child.* New York: The Free Press

Piburn, S. (Ed.). (1993). *The dalai lama: A policy of kindness: An anthology of writings by and about the dalai lama.* New York: Snow Lion Publications.

Radhakrishnan (1966). *Indian Philosophy Vol II.* New York: Humanities Press Inc.

Ratnagar, S. (2006). *Trading encounters: from the euphrates to the indus in the bronze age.* New York: Oxford University Press

Richardson, M. (1996). *Refusal of the shadow: Surrealism and the caribbean.* New York: Verso

Roberts, J.A.G. (1999). *A concise history of china.* Cambridge: Harvard University Press

Rodney, W. (1981). *How europe underdeveloped africa.* Washington: Howard University Press.

Rosaldo, M.Z. and Lamphere, L. (Eds.). (1985). *Woman, culture & society.* Stanford: Stanford University Press

Rosemont, F. (1978). *Andre breton what is surrealism?: Selected writings.* New York: Monad Press

Rudgley, R. (2000). *The lost civilizations of the stone age.* New York: Simon & Schuster

Russell, B. (1981). *The problems of philosophy.* New York: Oxford University Press

Safranski, R. (1998). *Heidegger: Between good and evil.* Cambridge: Harvard University Press

Samuels, W.D. (1977). *Five afro-caribbean voices in american culture. 1917-1929* Boulder: Belmont Books

Saro-Wiwa, K. (1985). *Songs in a time of war.* Port Harcourt: Saros International Publishers

Shapiro, B. (2005). *Porn generation: How social liberalism is corrupting our future.* Washington, D.C.: Regnery Publishing, Inc.

Shillington, K. (1989). *History of africa.* New York: St. Martin's Press

Sjoo, M. and Mor, B. (1987). *The great cosmic mother.* New York: Harper & Row

Smith, J.C. (1994). *Black firsts.* Washington: Visible Ink Press

Soyinka, W. (Ed.). (1975). *Poems of black africa.* New York: Hill and Wang

Spears, R. (Ed.). (1991). *West african folktales.* Evanston: Northwestern University Press

Stace, W.T. (1995). *The philosophy of hegel.* New York: Dover Publications, Inc.

Stein, M. (1998). *Jung's map of the soul: An introduction.* Chicago: Open Court Publishing Company

Strand, M. (Ed.). (1970). *New poetry of mexico.* New York: E.P. Dutton & Co., Inc.

Szwed, J.F. (1997). *Space is the place: The lives and times of sun ra.* New York: Pantheon Books

Talbot, M. (1992). *The holographic universe.* New York: Harper Perennial

Teilhard De Chardin, P. (1969). *Human energy.* London: William Collins Sons & Co., Ltd.

Tillich, P. (1952). *The courage to be.* London: Yale University Press

Turco, L. (1986). *The new book of forms: A handbook of poetics.* London: University Press of New England

Umeh, J.A. (1999). *After god is dibia: Igbo cosmology, healing, divination & sacred science in nigeria.* London: Karnac House

Valade, III, R.M. (1996). *The essential black literature guide.* New York: Visible Ink Press

van der Leeuw, G. (1963). *Religion in essence and manifestation: A study in phenomenology vols. 1 & 2.* New York: Harper & Row Publishers

van der Post, L. (1975). *Jung & the story of our time.* New York: Pantheon

Veach, D. (2001). *Atlanta review (Volume VII. Issue 2).* Atlanta: Poetry Atlanta

Welsh, L. and P. (2000). *Rock art of the south west: A visitor's companion.* Berkeley: Wilderness Press

West, C. (1999). *The cornel west reader.* New York: Basic *Civitas* Books

Westphal, M. (1987). *God, guilt and death: An existential phenomenology of religion.* Bloomington: Indiana University Press

Wilber, K. (2001). *Eye to eye: The quest for the new paradigm.* Boston: Shambhala

Wilber, K. (2000). *Integral psychology: Consciousness, spirit, psychology, therapy.*

London: Shambhala

Wilber, K. (2000). *One taste: Daily reflections on integral spirituality.* Boston: Shambhala

Wilber, K. (2000). *Sex, ecology, spirituality: The spirit of evolution.* Boston: Shambhala

Wilber, K. (1981). *Up from eden: A transpersonal view of human evolution.* Garden City, N.Y.: Anchor Press/Doubleday

Wiseman, B. and Groves, J. (2000). *Introducing levi-strauss and structural anthropology*. New York: Totem Books

Zee, A. (1999). *Fearful symmetry: The search for beauty in modern physics*. Princeton, N.J.: Princeton University Press

Mike Loutzenhiser lives in Boulder, Colorado, where he
studies, writes, paints, and works with the local
campaign for a Department of Peace.

www.ingramcontent.com/pod-product-compliance
Lightning Source LLC
Chambersburg PA
CBHW020428290526
45785CB00002B/747